HOT SPOT 3

Colin Granger
Katherine Stannett

Student's

MACMILLAN

Contents

1 Where I live

1 Presentation

a (1.02) Listen and read. What is special about the places where Sun and Lukas live?

Sun

Lukas

My name is Sun and I live in Dongguan County in China. People call Dongguan the *home of swimming* because many of China's top **divers** and swimmers come from here. There are good places to swim in the **creeks** along the Zhu River. Farmers sometimes swim to their fields because it is quicker than walking to the nearest bridge.

This is my e-pal Lukas. He lives in the Yukon in Canada and in the summer he sometimes sees bears in his garden. He always **claps** his hands when he leaves the house. He does this because bears usually walk away when they hear humans. Lukas doesn't have to worry in the winter because bears **hibernate** from October to April.

b Read again. Can you guess what the words in blue mean?

2 Comprehension

Read again. Answer these questions.

1 Dongguan County

1 Where does Sun live?
2 What do people call Dongguan?
3 Why do farmers sometimes swim to their fields?
4 Where does Lukas live?
5 What does Lukas sometimes see in his garden?
6 When do bears hibernate?

Grammar spot
Present simple

I **live** in Dongguan County in China.
Lukas **lives** in the Yukon in Canada.
What **do** people **call** Dongguan County?
Where **does** Lukas **live**?

Grammar page 98

❸ Grammar practice

a Make questions with *do* or *does*.

1 Where _____ Sun live?
2 Where _____ you come from?
3 What _____ bears do in winter?
4 Where _____ your friends go swimming?
5 Why _____ Lukas not have to worry about bears in winter?

b Then ask and answer with a classmate.

> Where does Sun live?

> She lives in Dongguan County.

Remember!
Remember the -(e)s!

Where do you live?
I live in …

Where do**es** he live?
He liv**es** in …

❹ Class poll

a What is special about where you live? Work in a small group and write ideas. Use a dictionary to help with new vocabulary. Then write your ideas on the board.

> There is a big forest and lots of sawmills.
> Lots of people work on farms.
> You can sometimes see deer.

b What are the best three ideas? Vote with your classmates.

❺ Pronunciation

a 〔1.03〕 Listen to this tongue twister.

/h/
Hedgehogs have to hibernate in their homes but humans have houses and don't have to.

b 〔1.04〕 Listen again and repeat. How fast can you say it?

❻ Listening

a 〔1.05〕 Listen to Rachel. Is her life different from yours?

> My name's Rachel and I'm Amish.

b 〔1.05〕 Listen again. Then write answers to the questions below. Use the words in the box.

> the USA   a simple, traditional life
> horse-drawn buggies   on their farms
> TVs, computers and mobile phones

1 Rachel lives in the USA.

1 Where does Rachel live?
2 What kind of life do Amish people like?
3 What have they not got?
4 How do they travel?
5 How do they help their neighbours?

❼ Check your English

a How much can you remember? Make sentences with the present simple.

1 Sun (live) …
2 People (call) Dongguan …
3 Lukas (live) …
4 Lukas (not worry) …
5 The Amish people (live) …
6 The Amish people (travel) …

b Do these things:

1 Write the name of a top diver or swimmer.
2 Draw a creek.
3 Clap your hands.
4 Think of two animals that hibernate.
5 Think of the name of one of your neighbours.
6 Think of something traditional in your country.

2 Charlie's busy week

① Presentation

a 1.06 Listen and read. Today is Monday. When are Charlie and his friends practising the sketch?

Mel	Here are the scripts. This is yours, Charlie, and this is mine. So when can we practise the sketch?
Charlie	Let's see. I'll look in my diary on my mobile.
Sophie	How about tomorrow after school?
Charlie	No, I'm sorry, I can't. I'm seeing the dentist on Tuesday.
Mel	Okay. Are you free on Wednesday?
Charlie	No, I'm going out with my family. We're going to the cinema.
Sophie	Right. How about on Thursday?
Charlie	Let's see. No, I'm afraid not. My sister's playing netball for the school team on Thursday and I'm watching the match.
Mel	So that leaves Friday. Are you free on Friday?
Charlie	Let's see. Oh no! We're going away for the weekend on Friday and we aren't coming back until Sunday night.
Sophie	But that's terrible! We're performing the sketch in class next Monday.
Charlie	How about now?
Mel	What? You're free now?
Charlie	Yes.
Sophie	Great! Let's practise the sketch right now. We haven't got a moment to lose.

b 1.06 Listen again. Then read the dialogue with your classmates.

Real English

Let's see.
How about tomorrow?
No, I'm afraid not.
We haven't got a moment to lose.

② Comprehension

When is Charlie doing what? Match the words in A with the times in B.

1 seeing the dentist – Tuesday

A		**B**	
1	seeing the dentist	**a**	Sunday night
2	going to the cinema	**b**	Wednesday
3	watching netball	**c**	Friday
4	going away	**d**	right now
5	coming back	**e**	next Monday
6	performing the sketch	**f**	Thursday
7	practising the sketch	**g**	Tuesday

Grammar spot
Present continuous for future arrangements

I'**m seeing** the dentist on Tuesday.

My sister'**s playing** netball for the school team on Thursday.

What **are** you **doing** on Wednesday?

I'**m going out** with my family.

👓 **Grammar page 98**

❸ Grammar practice

a Write questions using the present continuous.

1 When is Charlie seeing the dentist?

1 When/Charlie/see the dentist?
2 When/Charlie and his family/go/to the cinema?
3 When/Charlie's sister/play/netball?
4 When/Charlie and his family/go/away for the weekend?
5 When/they/come/back?
6 When/Mel, Charlie and Sophie/practise/their sketch?
7 When/they/perform/their sketch?

b Now ask and answer the questions.

When is Charlie seeing the dentist?

He's seeing the dentist on Tuesday.

❹ Speaking

a Invent some plans for the week. Choose one day when you don't have any plans. Don't show your classmate.

> *Monday – I'm meeting my friends.*
> *Tuesday – I'm watching TV.*
> *Wednesday – I'm going to the park.*
> *Thursday –*
> *Friday – I'm doing my homework.*
> *Saturday – I'm shopping.*
> *Sunday – I'm visiting my grandparents.*

b Now find out which day your classmate is free. Ask and answer questions.

Are you free on Friday?

No, I'm not. I'm doing my homework.

How about on Monday?

No, I'm afraid not. I'm meeting my friends.

❺ Pronunciation

a 🔊 **1.07** Listen to this chant.

I've got yours and you've got mine.

She's got his and he's got hers.

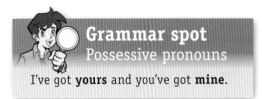
We've got theirs and they've got ours.

b 🔊 **1.07** Listen again and repeat. Notice the intonation of speech.

Grammar spot
Possessive pronouns

I've got **yours** and you've got **mine**.

👓 **Grammar page 98**

My English file

Write about your true plans for the rest of the week.

I'm playing basketball tomorrow.
I'm going shopping on Saturday morning.

❻ Check your English

a Complete with the present continuous of these verbs.

> help hang out wash go watch do have

A: What ¹_____ you _____ this evening?
B: I ²_____ a shower and ³_____ my hair. And then my sister and I ⁴_____ our favourite TV programme at nine o'clock. What about you? Are you ⁵_____ with your friends?
B: No, I'm not. My brother ⁶_____ away tomorrow and I ⁷_____ him get ready.

b Collect things from your classmates and put them on a desk. Can you remember who the things belong to? Make sentences.

This is his.

These are theirs.

3 The cheapest shirts in town

❶ Guessing

Look at the pictures. Choose the correct words.

1 The boy wants *to buy some jeans/to buy a shirt.*   **2** He *wants to/doesn't want to* buy a cheap shirt.

❷ Presentation

a (1.08) Listen and read. Which shirt does Oscar buy?

Oscar   Phoebe, do you like this shirt?
Phoebe   No. I don't like the pattern.
Oscar   But look. They're the cheapest shirts in town!
Phoebe   Yes, but they look horrible.

Phoebe   What about these?
Oscar   Yes, but how much are they?
Phoebe   They're £29.
Oscar   £29! They're much more expensive than the shirts in the sale.
Phoebe   Yes, but these shirts are much nicer.

Phoebe   What about these? They're cheaper than the blue shirts.
Oscar   What size are they?
Phoebe   They're large.
Oscar   No, those shirts are too big.

Oscar   Come on, Phoebe. I'm going to buy this. It's the right size and the right price.
Phoebe   But you can't buy that! It's the same as the shirt you've got on!
Oscar   Yes, and I like the shirt I've got on – that's why I'm buying it.

Real English

They're large.
It's the right size and the right price.

b (1.08) Listen again. Then read the dialogue with a classmate.

❸ Comprehension

Answer these questions about the dialogue in Activity 2.

1 Why doesn't Phoebe like the yellow shirt?
2 Why doesn't Oscar like the blue shirt?
3 What's wrong with the green shirt?
4 Why does Oscar like the brown shirt?

Remember!

The spelling changes in comparative and superlative adjectives:

big   bigger   biggest
tidy   tidier   tidiest

Grammar spot
Comparative/superlative

Comparative
These shirts are **cheaper** than the blue shirts.
These shirts are **more expensive** than the shirts in the sale.

Superlative
These are **the cheapest** shirts in town.
These are **the most expensive** shirts in town.

We can make comparatives stronger with **much**:
These shirts are **much** nicer.

 Grammar page 99

❹ Grammar practice

a Look at the pictures and make sentences using the comparative.

1 The yellow ball is bigger than the white ball.

1 yellow ball/white ball (big)
2 yellow ball/brown ball (small)
3 brown vase/green vase (cheap)
4 green vase/orange vase (expensive)

b Look at the pictures again and make sentences using the superlative.

1 The white ball is the smallest.

1 white ball (small)
2 brown ball (big)
3 brown vase (cheap)
4 green vase (expensive)

❺ Speaking

Make true sentences about things in the classroom with:

more interesting/most interesting
smaller/smallest   older/oldest   nicer/nicest
more comfortable/most comfortable
worse/worst   tidier/tidiest   messier/messiest
more beautiful/most beautiful   better/best

This book is more interesting than this book.

❻ Check your English

Complete the sentences about these T-shirts. Use the comparative or the superlative of the adjectives in brackets.

1 The red T-shirt is _____ than the green T-shirt. (expensive)
2 The green T-shirt is _____ than the blue T-shirt. (cheap)
3 The blue T-shirt is the _____ (big).
4 The green T-shirt is the _____ (small).
5 The blue T-shirt is the _____ (expensive).

4 Looking after your pet

1 Reading

a (1.09) Listen and read the quiz. Find these words. Do you know or can you guess what they mean?

treat bone aquarium sawdust stroke swish teach mice feed

Quiz Looking after your pet

1 Your pet dog is very good and you want to give it something special to eat. What is the best treat you can give it?

A a dog biscuit
B a chocolate bar
C a chicken bone

2 You read in a book that the best home for your gerbil is a glass aquarium. What do you put at the bottom of the aquarium?
A water **B** sawdust and cardboard
C nothing

3 You are stroking your cat. It is swishing its tail back and forth. What do you do?
A stop stroking it **B** stroke its tail
C continue stroking it

4 Your parrot looks bored. What can you teach your parrot to do?
A sing **B** fly **C** talk

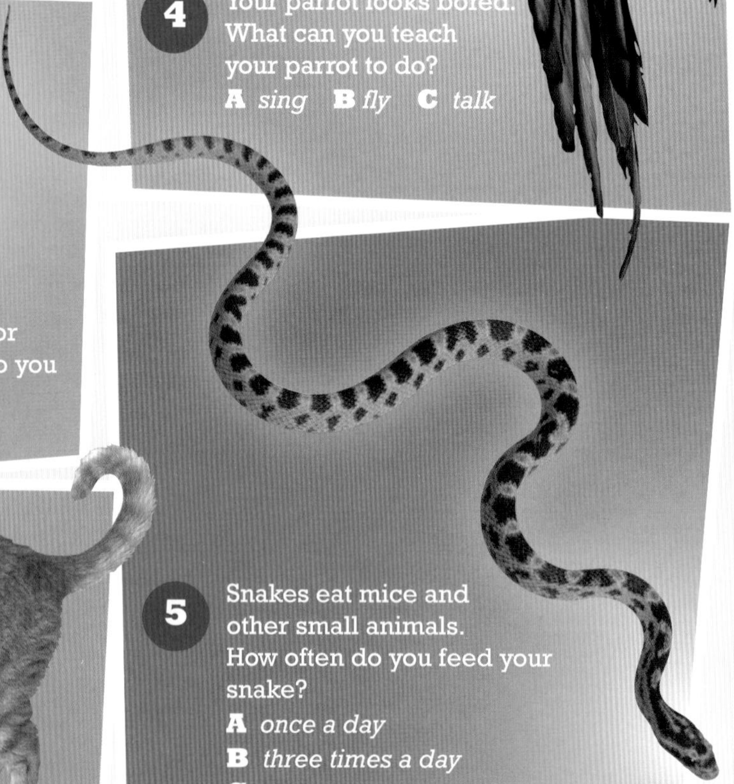

5 Snakes eat mice and other small animals. How often do you feed your snake?
A once a day
B three times a day
C once every two weeks

b Now complete the quiz. Write your answers.

② Listening

a 🔊 1.10 Listen to the answers to the quiz. Are your answers correct?

b 🔊 1.10 Listen again. What are the missing words?

1 Chicken bones are too s_____ and d_____.
2 Gerbils can make nests under the s_____ and c_____.
3 Cats are feeling a_____ or u_____ when they swish their t_____.
4 R_____ the same w_____ everyday until your parrot can s_____ it.
5 Don't f_____ your snake m_____ often than this.

③ Speaking

a Think of a pet animal and write the name on a piece of paper. Don't show your classmates.

A dog

b Guess what your classmate's pet animal is. Ask questions with *Do ...? Is ...? Can ...? Has ...?*

Do you give your pet biscuits?

Yes, I do.

Is your pet bigger than a mouse?

④ Writing

a Read below. Can you guess what kind of animal it is?

Looking after my pet

I talk to him every day.
I clean his cage every week.
I feed him small pieces of fruit and seeds.
I give him fresh water every day.
I put toys in his cage.

b Now choose an animal and write about how you look after it. Then get your classmates to guess what animal it is.

Looking after my pet
_____
I feed her once a day.
I give her biscuits and pet food.
I take her for a walk twice a day.

Who am I? game

Play with your classmates.

1 Think of a famous person.

3 Your classmates have 20 questions to guess who you are.

Do you live in Europe?

Are you a singer?

4 Answer their questions with short answers.

2 Write the person's name on a piece of paper.

Yes, I do.

No, I'm not.

Review

Check you can do these things.

1 I can use the present simple to talk about people and animals.
Complete these sentences with the present simple form of these verbs.

> clap   travel   live   leave   build   swim   hibernate

1 Sun _____ in China.
2 Farmers in Dongguan County, China, sometimes _____ to their fields.
3 When Lukas _____ his house, he _____ his hands.
4 Bears _____ in the winter.
5 Amish people _____ in horse-drawn buggies.

2 I can make and answer questions.

a Put the words into the correct order to make questions.

1 Lukas | his | does | clap | Why | hands?
2 Zhu | the | Where | River | is?
3 fields | do | their | swim | Why | to | farmers?
4 do | bears | winter | What | do | in?
5 people | travel | do | Amish | How?

b Then answer the questions.

3 I know the names of these four activities.
Write the activities. Use the initial letters to help you.

p _ _ _ n _ _ _ _ _ _

g _ t _ t _ _ c _ _ _ _ _

s _ _ t _ _ d _ _ _ _ _ _

g _ a _ _ _

4 **I can use the present continuous to talk about future arrangements.**

Use the present continuous to complete this dialogue.

Mum Eric, your room is a mess! Please tidy it up this afternoon.

Eric Oh, sorry Mum, I can't. I ¹_____ (play) football with Viv this afternoon.

Mum Well, what about Saturday morning then?

Eric No, that's impossible. I ²_____ (meet) my friends, Mark and Rama. We ³_____ (go) to the cinema.

Mum How about Saturday afternoon?

Eric Er, no, sorry. I ⁴_____ (practise) the sketch for school with Gemma on Saturday afternoon. We ⁵_____ (perform) it in front of the whole school on Monday morning.

Mum Well then, how about Sunday?

Eric I ⁶_____ (do) my homework on Sunday.

5 **I can talk about possessions.**

Use the correct possessive pronoun from the box to complete these sentences.

> yours   mine   his   hers   theirs   ours

1 This is my car. It's _____.

2 He's holding his bag. It's _____.

3 She's got her shoes. They're _____.

4 They've got your book. It's _____.

5 I can see their house. It's _____.

6 He's got our football. It's _____.

6 **I can compare things.**

Write sentences to compare the things. Use the adjective in brackets.

1 (expensive) The red car _____ than the green car. The blue car _____.

2 (big) The green hat is _____ than the pink hat. The orange hat is _____.

3 (cheap) The blue radio is _____ than the yellow radio. The black radio is _____.

4 (comfortable) The purple sofa is _____ than the grey sofa. The brown sofa is _____.

Extra special

Mystery European adventure

a Work in a small team.

b Look at the map and follow this journey around Europe. Use the key to help you. Write the names of the cities you visit.

1 Amsterdam

We're starting in London and then taking the train to ¹_____. Next, we're taking the ferry to ²_____. After that we're taking the plane to ³_____. Then we're taking the ferry to ⁴_____. After that we're taking the train to ⁵_____. Next, we're taking the coach to ⁶_____. Then we're taking the ferry to ⁷_____. Then we're taking the train to ⁸_____. After that we're taking the plane to ⁹_____. Next, we're taking the ferry to ¹⁰_____. Then we're taking the coach to ¹¹_____. After that, we're taking the train to ¹²_____. Then we're taking the plane to ¹³_____. And finally we're taking the ferry to ¹⁴_____.

c The winner is the first team to write the names of the 14 cities in the correct order.

d (1.11) Listen to the answers.

coach
plane
train
ferry

Oslo
Dublin
London Amsterdam
Paris
Geneva
Lisbon
Barcelona
Naples

Helsinki

Moscow

Gdansk

Vienna

Istanbul

Athens

Mini-project

1 Read Sam's poster. Compare his world with your own.

Me and my world

My family is …
My mum, my kid brother, my cousin Toby, my uncle and aunt and my cat Tickle.

My home is …
A flat in Hope Street, Liverpool. It's on the second floor and has got two bedrooms, a big living room, a kitchen and a bathroom.

My school is …
Crosby High School. It's a very big school with 1600 students. I'm in Year 9 and my form teacher is Miss Edwards.

My friends are …
Lex, Rich, Tony, Bof and Danny. They're all at the same school as me. Rich, Tony and Bof are in the same year as me and Lex and Danny are in Year 10.

My favourite sports are …
Football, skateboarding and running. I'm good at running and football but I'm terrible at skateboarding.

Sam

2 Make a poster about your world.

3 Exchange posters with your classmates. Find out about their world.

Lesson objectives
● **Talking about the past**
● **Talking about sports**

5 Sports day

❶ Vocabulary

1.12 Match the sports with the pictures.

swimming race   javelin   100-metre race
obstacle course   long jump

❷ Presentation

1.13 Listen and read. Why is Charlie unhappy?

Charlie	Hello.
Mel	Hi Charlie! How was Sports day?
Charlie	Oh, not so good. What a disaster!
Mel	But you're really good at sport! What happened?
Charlie	I ran fast and I won the 100-metre race.
Mel	Brilliant!
Charlie	My team swam well in the swimming race. We didn't win, but we got a medal.

Mel	Cool!
Charlie	I threw the javelin 28 metres and everyone cheered.
Mel	Well done!
Charlie	I jumped 4.8 metres and I broke the school long jump record!
Mel	Wow, Charlie, that's amazing!
Charlie	The last race was the obstacle course. I didn't see the rope and I fell over …

… I twisted my ankle and broke my arm. No more sport for six weeks!

❸ Comprehension

1.13 Listen and read again. Answer these questions.

1   The swimming race.

1   In which sport did Charlie win a medal?
2   How far did Charlie throw the javelin?
3   How far did Charlie jump?
4   What was the last race?
5   What happened to Charlie in the last race?

Grammar spot
Past simple

I **jumped** 4.8 metres and I **broke** the school record!
We **didn't win** but we **got** a medal.

📖 Grammar page 99

Study tip
Past simple

Add irregular verbs to your verb table.

break – broke	*get – got*
win – won	*fall – fell*
swim – swam	*run – ran*

❹ Grammar practice

a What did they do on Sports Day?
Look at the chart. Make sentences about
Charlie's friends.

Ryan didn't swim in the swimming race.
He ran in the 800-metre race.

	swimming race	800-metre race	javelin
Ryan	✗	✓	✗
Sophie	✗	✓	✓

	long jump	obstacle course	medal
Ryan	✓	✓	✓
Sophie	✓	✗	✗

b Work in pairs. Ask and answer about
Ryan and Sophie.

Did Ryan swim in the swimming race?

No, he didn't.

❺ Listening

🔊 **1.14** Listen to Charlie talking about his
weekend. Put the phrases in the correct order.

Last weekend, Charlie …

___	bought a tennis racket	___	talked about cycling
___	looked at a bike	___	visited an exhibition
___	read a book	___	did his homework
_1_	watched TV	___	went to his uncle's

❻ Speaking

a What did you do last weekend? Read the
questions and write answers about yourself.

Did you buy anything?
What did you buy?
Did you read a book or a magazine?
Did you watch TV?
What did you watch?
Did you visit a friend/a relative?
What did you talk about?
Did you do your homework?

b Work in pairs. Find out about your friend's
weekend. Ask the questions above and make
notes.

c Tell another classmate about your friend's
weekend.

Last weekend, Sophie bought a CD. She …

❼ Pronunciation

a 🔊 **1.15** Listen to this tongue twister.

/v/ /w/
Victoria Wells won one hundred volleyball
victories and was wonderful at windsurfing.

b 🔊 **1.16** Listen again and repeat. How fast can
you say it?

❽ Check your English

Use the past simple of the verbs in brackets to
complete Mel's diary.

Last Saturday I ¹_____ (visit) Charlie and then we
²_____ (go) to the new café in town for lunch.
After lunch, I ³_____ (buy) some trainers and
Charlie ⁴_____ (get) a DVD of his favourite film.
Then we ⁵_____ (go) to Charlie's house and
⁶_____ (watch) the DVD.

6 What were you doing?

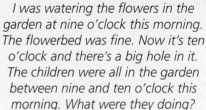
Martha

❶ Vocabulary

1.17 Find these things in the picture.

> hammock   clothes line   flowerbed   bone   flowerpot

❷ Presentation

1.18 Look at the picture and listen to Martha Gloom. Why is she angry?

> *I was watering the flowers in the garden at nine o'clock this morning. The flowerbed was fine. Now it's ten o'clock and there's a big hole in it. The children were all in the garden between nine and ten o'clock this morning. What were they doing?*

Sam

Pam

Rudolph

Vincent

a

b

c

d

e

Helga

Mandy

❸ Comprehension

a Look at the picture again. What were the Glooms doing this morning? Write the name.

1 Helga

1 _____ was reading a magazine.
2 _____ was listening to music.
3 _____ were climbing a tree.
4 _____ was sleeping in a hammock.
5 _____ was skipping.
6 _____ was burying a bone.

b **1.19** Listen and check.

Grammar spot
Past continuous

He **was listening** to music.
They **were climbing** a tree.

🎧 Grammar page 100

④ Grammar practice

a 〔1.20〕 Look at the picture in Activity 2 and listen to Vincent. Then correct his mistakes. Use the phrases in the box.

1 Helga wasn't mowing the lawn. She was reading a magazine.

mow the lawn   water the plants   hang up the washing   play with toys   sleep

1 Helga _____. **2** Rudolph _____. **3** Mandy _____. **4** Sam and Pam _____. **5** Bonehead _____.

b 〔1.21〕 Listen and check.

Grammar spot
Past continuous

Negative
Helga **wasn't mowing** the lawn.
Sam and Pam **weren't playing** with toys.

Questions
Were you **having** a shower? Yes, I **was**.
Was she **doing** her homework? No, she **wasn't**.

〔👀 Grammar page 100〕

⑤ Speaking

a Complete the chart about what you were doing yesterday. Use these or your own ideas.

sleep   eat breakfast/lunch/dinner/a snack
do homework   play football/tennis
talk on the phone   watch TV   get up
have a shower   have a lesson

7.30 am	*I was eating breakfast.*
10.00 am	
11.30 am	
5.30 pm	
8.00 pm	
10.00 pm	

b Work in pairs. Find out what your classmate was doing yesterday.

〔 *Were you having a shower at 7.30 yesterday?* 〕

〔 *No, I wasn't. I was eating breakfast.* 〕

⑥ Pronunciation

〔1.22〕 Listen and practise saying the weak forms of *was* /wəz/ and *were* /wə/.

1 I **was** playing tennis yesterday.
2 They **were** doing their homework.
3 Sarah **was** working with him.
4 We **were** eating breakfast.

⑦ Game

a Work in pairs. Look at the picture in Activity 2 for one minute.

b Now close your books. Ask and answer about the Glooms.

〔 *Was Rudolph mowing the lawn?* 〕

〔 *No, he wasn't. He was listening to music.* 〕

〔 *Correct!* 〕

⑧ Check your English

Choose the correct words and make sentences.

1 I *was/were* doing my homework at six o'clock last night.
2 *Was/Were* they watching TV yesterday afternoon?
3 Sara and Fred *wasn't/weren't* playing tennis this morning, they *was/were* taking the dog for a walk.
4 Last Sunday afternoon we were *sit/sitting* on the beach, *eat/eating* ice cream.

7 Amazing stories

Lesson objective
Telling a story in the past

1 Presentation

1.23 Listen and read. Match the photos with the emails.

TRUE STORIES PAGE

Have you got an amazing story for us?
Send an email to Teen Dreams and tell us your stories.

Get Mail   Write   Contacts   Reply   Forward   Delete   Print

1

Hi Teen Dreams!

Last Wednesday I was playing football with my school. It was a very important match and the score was 1-1. I was running towards the ball when I fell. My football boot came off and flew through the air. It hit the ball and the ball went into the goal. Just then, the referee blew his whistle and the game ended. Our team won the match! My football boot was the hero of the match! It was very funny!

Tony

Get Mail   Write   Contacts   Reply   Forward   Delete   Print

2

Dear Teen Dreams!

Last Saturday morning, my mum was mowing the lawn and my dad was at work. I was doing my homework in my room when I heard our dog, Bobo. He was barking loudly in the kitchen. I ran into the kitchen and saw a lot of smoke. The saucepan was on fire and Bobo was trying to tell me. I called my mum and we put out the fire. Bobo saved our lives! We were very lucky.

Sally

Get Mail   Write   Contacts   Reply   Forward   Delete   Print

3

Hi Teen Dreams!

I was shopping with my friend. We were looking at some CDs in a music shop. I was listening to some music when I heard a loud noise. It sounded like an alarm. I shouted, 'Fire! Fire!' and everyone started to run out of the shop. Then I realised that it wasn't an alarm, it was the music. It was so embarrassing!

Freya

a

b

c

2 Comprehension

Can you remember? Try to answer these questions from memory.

Sally   Bobo   Tony   Freya

1 Sally

1 Who was doing their homework?
2 Who was listening to music?
3 Who shouted, 'Fire! Fire!'?
4 Who was playing football?
5 Who was barking loudly?

Grammar spot
Past continuous and
past simple with *when*

I **was running** towards the ball *when* I **fell**.
I **was listening** to some music *when* I **heard** a loud noise.

Grammar page 100

❸ Grammar practice

a Use the past continuous or past simple of the verbs in brackets to complete this story.

1 was watching
2 heard

I ¹_____ (watch) TV when I ²_____ (hear) a strange noise outside. I ³_____ (go) into the garden. I ⁴_____ (look) around the garden when a cat ⁵ _____ (run) into my house. I ⁶_____ (run) after the cat when the doorbell ⁷_____ (ring). It ⁸_____ (be) my neighbour, Fred. He ⁹_____ (look) for his cat. I ¹⁰_____ (talk) to Fred when the cat ¹¹_____ (run) out of my house and into Fred's garden.

b (1.24) Listen and check.

❹ Vocabulary

Find words from the emails in Activity 1 to match these pictures.

1 whistle

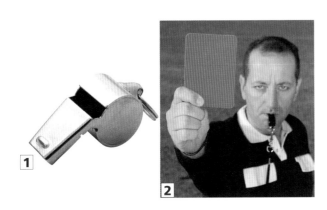

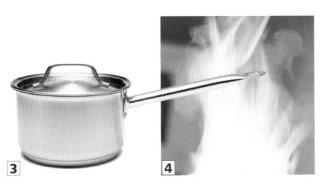

❺ Writing

a Look at the phrases below and complete Ted's letter to Teen Dreams. Use the past continuous and the past simple.

1 I was at home in the morning

at home in the morning/ get ready

very late/really angry/ get into car

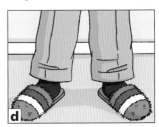

walk/start/point

wear

Hello Teen Dreams

This is my true story. I ¹_____ and I ²_____ for school. I ³_____ and my mum ⁴_____ with me. I ⁵_____ very quickly. I ⁶_____ into the classroom when my friend ⁷_____ to laugh. He ⁸_____ at my feet. I ⁹_____ my slippers! How embarrassing!

Ted

b (1.25) Now listen and check.

My English file

Make up your own amazing story.
● Where were you?
● What were you doing?
● What happened?

I was in my room listening to music. My sister...

❻ Check your English

Use the prompts to make sentences with *when*.

1 I was walking the dog when I found a purse.

1 walk the dog/find a purse
2 eat a sandwich/break my tooth
3 ride my bike/fall off
4 do my homework/fall asleep

8 My hero

① Reading

a (1.26) Read Sara's project about Aimee Mullins. Why is Aimee famous?

Aimee is also a model.

Aimee has special legs for running. She says, 'My brother calls them 'RoboCop legs'!

My hero
by Sara Chester

My hero is Aimee Mullins. Aimee was born in 1976 in Pennsylvania, USA. She's famous now as an athlete, an actress and a model but the beginning of her life was very difficult.

When she was born, Aimee had a problem with her legs. When she was one, she had a double amputation. This means that doctors cut off both her legs below her knees. However, Aimee got some artificial legs and she learnt to walk and then to run and jump!

Aimee loved sports at school. She skied and she played American football, softball and volleyball. She also studied hard. In 1995 she went to Georgetown University in Washington DC.

At university Aimee was a very good student and she trained hard at sports as well. She enjoyed athletics and she ran in races against able-bodied students. She broke records for the 100-metre race and the long jump.

Now Aimee is the President of the Women's Sports Foundation. She's an inspiration for sports people around the world.

Aimee is my hero because she didn't give up. She tried hard and achieved a lot. She's an amazing person!

b Read again. Then answer these questions about Aimee.

1 What happened to her when she was one?
2 What sports did Aimee play at school?
3 When did she go to university?
4 What sports did Aimee do at university?
5 Why is she Sara's hero?

❷ Speaking

Work in pairs. Look at the information below. Choose one person and tell your classmate about him/her.

> Orlando Bloom was born in …

Orlando Bloom

- born in 1977 in Kent, England
- had a lot of problems at school because he was dyslexic
- left home at 16 to study drama
- broke his back in 1998 but recovered quickly
- became famous as Legolas in 'The Lord of the Rings' trilogy

Bethany Hamilton

- born in 1990 in Hawaii
- loved swimming and surfing
- won first surfing competition at the age of 8
- a shark attacked her in October 2003 and bit off her left arm
- went surfing again just three weeks after the shark attack
- won the NSSA surfing championships in 2005

❸ Listening

a 🔊1.27 Listen to Adam talk about Bethany Hamilton. He makes three mistakes. Can you spot the mistakes? Use the information in Activity 2 to help you.

b 🔊1.28 Listen and check.

❹ Writing

a Who is your hero? Think of a person you admire. It can be a famous person, a friend or someone in your family.

b Make some notes about your hero.
- Where and when was your hero born?
- What did your hero do?
- What did your hero achieve?
- Why is this person a hero for you?

c Now write about your hero.

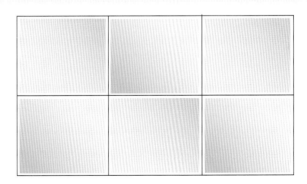

> My hero is my father. He was born in …

Writing tip

Try to use these words to link sentences together:

however	*The doctors cut off her legs. **However,** she got some artificial legs…*
but	*She's famous now as an athlete **but** the beginning of her life was very difficult.*
as well	*At university, Aimee was a very good student and she trained hard at sports **as well.***
because	*Aimee is my hero **because** she didn't give up.*

Past simple bingo

a Choose six verbs from this list. Write the past simple form in the grid.

> run win swim get throw break do
> read buy go fly blow see put hear
> have learn study cut enjoy leave

b Listen to your teacher. When you hear a verb in your grid, put a cross through it. Shout 'Bingo!' when all six verbs are crossed through. The first person to shout 'Bingo!' is the winner.

Review

Check you can do these things.

1 I know the names of these sports.
Write the sports. Use the initial letters to help you.

100-m_ _ _ _ r _ _ _

o _ _ _ _ _ _ _ _ c _ _ _ _ _

s _ _ _ _ _ _ _

l _ _ _ j _ _ _

j _ _ _ _ _ _

2 I know the past simple irregular form of ten verbs.
Write the past simple form of these irregular verbs.

1 run   **6** get
2 win   **7** fall
3 swim   **8** do
4 throw   **9** read
5 break   **10** buy

3 I can use the past simple to talk about finished actions in the past.

a Complete this text about Charlie. Use the past simple tense of the verbs in brackets.

Last weekend Charlie ¹_____ (not do) any sport. He ²_____ (watch) football on TV on Friday night. On Saturday he ³_____ (read) a book about swimming. He ⁴_____ (do) his homework and then he ⁵_____ (visit) his uncle. On Sunday he ⁶_____ (buy) a new tennis racket and ⁷_____ (go) to his local museum.

b What did you do yesterday? Write three sentences with the past simple.

I went to school.

4 **I can use the past continuous to describe past activities.**

Look at the pictures. Write sentences about what the children were doing at eight o'clock this morning.

1   Paul, Sarah and Alice w_____ s_____ on a bench.
2   Sarah w_____ r_____ a book.
3   Alice w_____ l_____ to music.
4   Marie w_____ s_____ .
5   Jim w_____ c_____ a tree.
6   Paul w_____ s_____ .

5 **I can ask and answer questions about the past.**

What were the Glooms doing this morning? Ask and answer.

> *Was Helga mowing the lawn?*

> *No, she wasn't. She was reading a magazine.*

1   Helga/mow lawn?
2   Rudolph/water plants?
3   Mandy/hang up washing?
4   Bonehead/sleep?
5   Sam and Pam/play with toys?

6 **I can tell a story in the past with the past simple and the past continuous.**

Choose the correct form to complete this story.

Last Sunday I ¹*watched/was watching* TV
when I ²*heard/was hearing* a strange noise.
I ³*switched/was switching* off the TV and
⁴*ran/was running* upstairs. My little sister
⁵*listened/was listening* to music on her MP3 player.
She ⁶*sang/was singing* with the music!

Extra reading
Turn to page 92 and read an extract from *Robinson Crusoe*.

Extra special

Mini-play

Look at the picture. What do you think the children are doing?

a (1.29) Listen and read the first part of the play. What do you think happens at the end?

Danny Great. The tents are up! One tent for the boys and one tent for the girls.

Maria Yes, this is brilliant! The fire is burning and the food is cooking. Our first camping trip! Now where are the others?

Sandra Hi guys! Sorry we're late. It's all Ben's fault.

Ben No, it isn't my fault; it's yours. You forgot the torch!

Sandra Yes, and you forgot the blankets!

Maria OK, OK, guys! We're all here now.

Ben Actually the real problem was Lucy.

Maria Your little sister?

Sandra	Yes. She really wanted to come too. But she's too young for camping.
Ben	She's at home with Mum and Dad.
Danny	Anyway … I'm hungry! Let's have some food.
Sandra	Great idea.
Maria	Right, sausages and beans for everyone. Mmm, delicious.
Sandra	Wow. Look at the stars. They're beautiful!
Danny	Yes. And it's so quiet.
Ben	It's quite dark here.
Maria	Yes. No electric lights. This is the real natural world!
Sandra	Well, Maria, it's not actually the real natural world. It's your garden!
Maria	OK, OK. But it's still exciting!
Sandra	Did you hear that?
Danny	What?
Maria	I think I heard something.
Ben	What did you hear?
Maria	I don't know. A strange sound.
Sandra	I didn't hear anything.
Danny	Did you hear that?
Sandra	Yes, I did.
Ben	Oh, don't be silly. It was nothing. Just a … sound.
Danny	I'm not scared.
Sandra	No, I'm not scared. I'm definitely not scared.
All	Aaagggh!
Ben	OK everyone. Calm down, calm down. It's probably a bird.
Sandra	Or a fox.
Danny	I've got a really good idea.
Maria	What?
Danny	Let's go and get Mum and Dad.
Maria	No way!
Sandra	That sound's coming from your tent, boys!
Ben	Right! That's it! Come on, Danny, we're going in!

b (1.30) Now listen to the last part. Did you guess the ending?

c (1.31) Listen again to the whole dialogue. Then read with your classmates.

> ## Memory challenge
> Learn your lines by heart.

Mini-project

1 Read Jack's fact sheet. Does your school have any similar after-school sports clubs?

Sports at my school

We do lots of sports at my school. In the summer, we do cricket, rounders and athletics. In the winter we do football, rugby and gymnastics. My favourite sport is gymnastics.
We also have after-school sports clubs.

I do karate and netball after school.
Every summer we have a sports day at our school. The students take part in lots of different sports competitions and the winners get medals.

Jack

2 Write about sports at your school. Draw pictures or use photos from magazines to illustrate your fact sheet.

9 In my life

1 Presentation

a **1.32** Listen and read. Find the things Eva talks about in the pictures.

My first years

Have you ever visited a castle?
Have you ever visited a zoo?
Have you ever lived in an igloo?

I've visited a castle,
I've visited a zoo,
But I haven't lived in an igloo.

I've travelled on a bus,
I've travelled on a train,
But I've never been on an aeroplane.

I've eaten frogs' legs,
I've eaten spinach leaves,
But I've never eaten smelly cheese.

I've listened to rock,
I've listened to pop,
But I've never danced to hip hop.

I've taken lots of exams,
I've taken lots of tests,
But I haven't climbed Mount Everest.

Eva

b **1.32** Listen again. Practise saying the poem.

Grammar spot
Present perfect: *ever, never*

Have you **ever visited** a castle?
Yes, I **have**./No, I **haven't**.
I**'ve eaten** spinach leaves.
I **haven't climbed** Mount Everest.
I**'ve never been** on an aeroplane.

👀 Grammar page 101

Remember!

Full form	Short form
I **have**	I**'ve**
I **have not**	I **haven't**

❷ Grammar practice

a Complete three of these phrases to make true sentences about yourself.

I've never eaten …	I've travelled on a …
I haven't tasted …	I've been to …
I've listened to …	I haven't lived in …
I've visited …	I've never danced to …

1 I've never eaten spinach.
2 I've been to Italy.
3 I've never danced to hip hop.

b Read your sentences to your classmates. Try to find someone with one or two sentences like yours.

Study tip
Remembering past participles

Write down verbs in lists of regular and irregular verbs

Regular	Irregular
visit – visited	*be – been*
listen – listened	*eat – eaten*
taste – tasted	*take – taken*

❸ Pronunciation

🔊 **1.33** Listen and practise saying these verbs.

/ɪd/ visited shouted started ended
/d/ travelled listened climbed played
/t/ danced worked helped watched

❹ Speaking

a 🔊 **1.34** Listen and read these questions.

Experiences Have you ever …

1 played tennis?

4 seen a rainbow?

2 been to London?

5 eaten Chinese food?

3 swum in the sea?

6 won a prize?

b Now ask and answer the questions with a classmate.

Have you ever played tennis?

No, I haven't. or *Yes, I have.*

❺ Class poll

🔊 **1.35** Listen to the questions in Activity 4 again. Put your hand up for all the things you have done. Write the results on the board.

	Yes, I have	No, I haven't
1 Tennis	9	11
2 London	…	

❻ Check your English

Complete with *have, haven't, ever, never*.

A: Have you [1]_____ eaten Mexican food?
B: No, I've [2]_____ eaten Mexican food, but I [3]_____ eaten Spanish food. Have you [4]_____ eaten Spanish food?
A: No, I [5]_____.

10 An amazing life

Lesson objective

Talking about experiences you have had in your life

❶ Presentation

a 1.36 Listen and read. Find the things Mandy talks about in the picture.

Sam	Wow. Look at these!
Mandy	Yes, Grandpa's been all over the world. Look. He's ridden an elephant in India.
Pam	Cool. Has he ever climbed Mount Everest?
Mandy	No, he's never climbed Mount Everest. But he's climbed Mount Kilimanjaro and that's the highest mountain in Africa.
Pam	Wow! What else has he done?
Mandy	Well, he's written lots of books and he's made films.
Sam	Has he written any children's books?
Mandy	No, he hasn't written any children's books. But he's written lots of travel books. And he's met a king and a queen and he's broken …
Sam	His leg!
Mandy	No, he hasn't broken his leg. He's broken world records. Look. He's sailed around the world in 80 days and he's skied down Mont Blanc. Yes, Grandpa has had a really amazing life.
Pam	Umm. No wonder he's tired.

b 1.36 Listen again. Then read the dialogue with your classmates.

Real English

Cool
No wonder …

❷ Class poll

What do you think is the most amazing thing Gordon Gloom has done in his life? Vote and write the results on the board.

ridden an elephant – 2
climbed Mount Kilimanjaro – 5

Grammar spot
Present perfect

Has he ever **climbed** Mount Everest?
Yes, he **has.**/No, he **hasn't.**

He**'s ridden** an elephant in India.
He **hasn't written** any children's books.

🎧 Grammar page 101

3 Grammar practice

Look at the picture in Activity 1. Make sentences with *He has* or *He hasn't* and these words:

sailed written ridden skied
broken made met been

children's books, down Mont Blanc, an elephant, films, to lots of countries, around the world, kings and queens, his leg

He's sailed around the world.

He hasn't written children's books.

Remember!

Full form	*Short form*
He/She **has**	He/She**'s**
He/She **has not**	He/She **hasn't**

4 Listening

a 1.37 Listen and then fill in the missing words.

sailed been rode flew sailed
been flown took ridden

Sam	Is it true? Have you _____ an elephant?
Gordon	Yes, I _____ an elephant in India in 1948.
Pam	And have you _____ around the world?
Gordon	Yes, I _____ around the world in 1952. It _____ me eighty days.
Sam	Have you ever _____ to the moon?
Gordon	No, I haven't _____ to the moon. But I have _____ across the Pacific. Look, I _____ across the Pacific Ocean in this plane in 1937.
Pam, Sam	Wow. You are brave, Grandpa.

b 1.37 Listen again and check your answers.

Grammar spot
Present perfect and past simple

Have you **ridden** an elephant?
Yes, I **rode** an elephant in India **in 1948**.

Have you **sailed** around the world?
Yes, I **sailed** around the world **in 1952**.

Grammar page 101

5 Grammar practice

a Complete the dialogue with the correct form of the verb in brackets.

1 ridden, rode

1	(ride)	**Sam**	Have you _____ an elephant?
		Gordon	Yes, I _____ an elephant in 1948.
2	(broke)	**Pam**	Have you _____ a world record?
		Gordon	Yes, I _____ a world record in 1952.
3	(meet)	**Sam**	Have you _____ a king and queen?
		Gordon	Yes, I _____ a king and queen in 1960.
4	(fly)	**Pam**	Have you _____ across the Pacific?
		Gordon	Yes, I _____ across the Pacific in 1937.
5	(ski)	**Sam**	Have you _____ down Mont Blanc?
		Gordon	Yes, I _____ down Mont Blanc in 1977.
6	(climb)	**Pam**	Have you _____ Mount Kilimanjaro?
		Gordon	Yes, I _____ Mount Kilimanjaro in 1982.

b 1.38 Listen and check.

6 Song

1.39 Find the song *Have You Ever Seen the Rain?* on page 90.

7 Check your English

a Ask and answer questions about your classmate's experiences.

1 (travel) on a plane
2 (be) to England
3 (ride) a horse
4 (break) a leg

Have you travelled on a plane?

Yes, I have. I travelled on a plane last year.

b Now write sentences about you and your classmate's experiences.

I haven't travelled on a plane.
Monica has travelled on a plane.
She travelled on a plane last year.

11 My latest news

❶ Guessing

Phoebe is writing about things that have happened to her recently. Look at the picture. Can you guess her news?

❷ Presentation

1.40 Listen and read. How many pieces of news does Phoebe tell her cousin in Australia?

Get Mail Write Contacts Reply Forward Delete Print

Hi Sandra,

I hope things are good for you in Australia. I've got a lot of news for you! I've just started my new school and the uniform is cool. It's purple! And guess what? I've changed my hairstyle. Now my hair is really short. But my best news is that our cat Bonny has just had three kittens. They're really gorgeous!

Oscar is fine. He's really happy at the moment because he's just bought an MP3 player with his birthday money. He listens to it all the time and he can't hear anything I say. Annoying!

Mum and Dad are fine too. They've been really busy with DIY. They've just painted the kitchen. Dad isn't very happy because he's hurt his back. Mum has found a new job at a vet's. She's very happy because she really loves animals!

I have to go now – my best pal, Julie, has just invited me to a sleepover and I have to get ready and pack my bag!

Please write with all your news!

Phoebe

Do u fancy a sleepover tonite at mine ??? Julie

Real English

guess what?   pal
Annoying!   gorgeous

Text language
do u (= do you) tonite (= tonight)

Grammar spot
Present perfect: *just*

I**'ve** *just* **started** my new school.
Bonnie **has** *just* **had** three kittens.

📖 Grammar page 101

❸ Grammar practice

a Match the words in A with the words in B to make sentences using the present perfect.

> *I've just started my new school.*

	A		B
1	I just (start)	**a**	an MP3 player.
2	I (change)	**b**	his back.
3	Bonny just (have)	**c**	really busy.
4	Oscar just (buy)	**d**	my hairstyle.
5	Mum and Dad (be)	**e**	kittens.
6	They just (paint)	**f**	a new job at a vet's.
7	My dad (hurt)	**g**	me to a sleepover.
8	Mum (find)	**h**	the kitchen.
9	Julie just (invite)	**i**	my new school.

b 🔘 1.41 Listen and check.

❹ Listening

a 🔘 1.42 Listen. What news is Oscar telling his friend?

b 🔘 1.42 Listen again. Answer these questions.

1 What has Oscar just spent?
2 What did he buy?
3 Was it expensive?
4 Where did he buy it?
5 How many songs can it hold?
6 How many songs has Oscar put on it?

Grammar spot
Present perfect and past simple

I've **just spent** my birthday money.
What **did** you **buy**?
I **bought** an MP3 player.

❺ Speaking

Work with a classmate. Make a dialogue with the words in the boxes. Complete it with your own answer.

> *I've just been shopping.*

> *What did you buy?*

> *I bought a magazine.*

A: I've just …

> been shopping   won a prize   read a book
> seen a film   had a drink   played a game

B: What did you …?

> buy   win   read   see   have   play

A: I …

> bought   won   read   saw   had   played

My English file
My latest news

Write a dialogue between you and your friend.

My latest news

Me: Guess what! I've just been to a restaurant.
Karl: Cool. What did you eat?
Me: I had pizza.
Karl: Was it good?
Me: It was great.
Karl: What did you have for dessert?
Me: I had ice cream.

❻ Check your English

a Complete with the present perfect of the verb in brackets.

1 I ____ just ____ a T-shirt. (buy)
2 My cat ____ just ____ kittens. (have)
3 My friend ____ just ____ a new school. (start)
4 We ____ our house. (paint)
5 My dad ____ a new job. (find)

b Now write questions about the above with the past simple.

1 *Where did you buy it?*

12 Sumeo's story

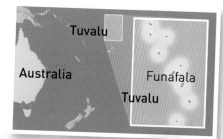

Tuvalu
Australia
Funafala
Tuvalu

❶ Reading

a 1.43 Listen and read about the Tuvaluan island of Funafala. Why do you think people on the island are afraid for its future?

Tuvalu fears for its future

1

My name is Sumeo and I live on the tiny island of Funafala in the South Pacific. This is my house. As you can see our house is very close to the sea. It isn't good to live close to the sea on Funafala because the land is very low. Sometimes the sea floods our island.

2

Two families have just left our island to live in New Zealand. One of these was my aunt and uncle's family. I am very sad because my cousins live so far away from Funafala. Now there are only five families on the island.

3

All the men on my island are fishermen. We have just brought a big net of fish back to the island. We share everything on my island and now we are going to share the fish between the five families. Fish is our main food on Funafala. We also eat chicken, pork and vegetables.

4

We have our own language in Tuvalu and we have our own songs and dances too. We are happy tonight but we are often sad when we think of the future.

b Read again. Are these sentences true or false?

1 True

1 Funafala is a tiny island.
2 The land on Funafala is very high.
3 All the men are farmers.

4 Sumeo's uncle and aunt live in New Zealand.
5 There are only two families on Funafala.
6 They are sad tonight.

❷ Listening

a (1.44) Listen to the interview with Sumeo. Then answer these questions.

1 Why is Sumeo's house on stilts?
2 Why have Sumeo's uncle and aunt left the island?
3 What food do they eat on Funafala?
4 Why are they happy tonight?

b (1.44) Listen again and check.

❸ Speaking

a (1.45) Look at the pictures in Activity 1 and listen. Think about the answers.

b Now play a quiz game. Get into small teams and write five questions to ask another team.

c Then close your books and ask and answer your questions. You get one point for every correct answer.

> *Why is Sumeo's house on stilts?*
>> *Because it's very close to the sea.*

❹ Writing

Write a paragraph about the island of Funafala. Try to use as many of these words as you can.

> tiny   South Pacific   houses   close to the sea
> land   low   stilts   afraid of   two families
> floods   New Zealand   afraid for the future
> five   fishermen   net   fish   share
> main food   chicken   pork   vegetables

Funafala

Funafala is a tiny island in the South Pacific. The island is ...

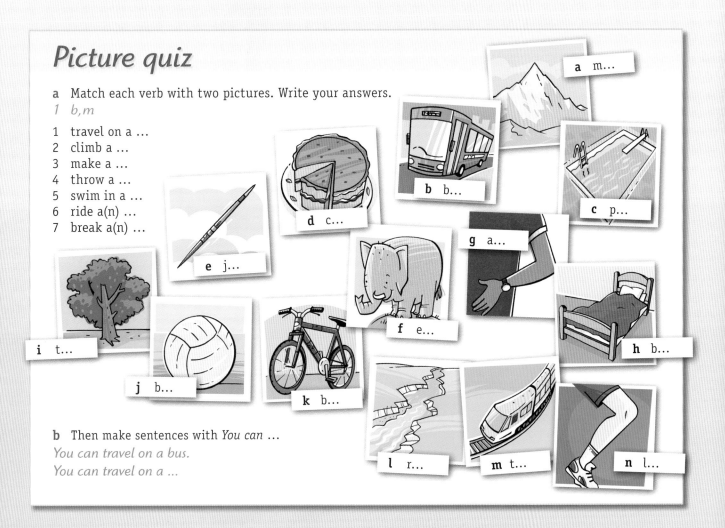

Picture quiz

a Match each verb with two pictures. Write your answers.
1 b,m

1 travel on a ...
2 climb a ...
3 make a ...
4 throw a ...
5 swim in a ...
6 ride a(n) ...
7 break a(n) ...

a m...
b b...
c p...
d c...
e j...
f e...
g a...
h b...
i t...
j b...
k b...
l r...
m t...
n l...

b Then make sentences with *You can* ...
You can travel on a bus.
You can travel on a ...

Review

Check you can do these things.

1 I know the past participle of some irregular verbs.

Find the present perfect form of five verbs in this word square.

t	o	s	k	t	t	s	h
w	i	n	d	w	a	a	e
b	h	b	r	o	k	e	n
e	a	t	e	n	e	w	a
e	t	s	e	e	n	a	r
n	e	g	o	e	d	s	t

2 I can talk about experiences using the present perfect.

Complete the questions about Eva. Then answer with *Yes, she has.* or *No, she hasn't.*

1 Has she ever visited a castle?   Yes, she has.

1 visit castle
2 live in an igloo
3 travel on a bus
4 be on an aeroplane
5 eat spinach
6 listen to rock
7 dance to hip hop
8 climb Mount Everest

3 I can use the past simple and the present perfect.

a Complete the dialogue with the correct word from the box.

made   wrote   skied   met   made   skied   written   met

Sam Is it true? Have you ¹_____ a book?
Gordon Yes, I ²_____ four travel books in 1948.
Pam And have you ³_____ a king and queen?
Gordon Yes, I ⁴_____ a king and queen in 1960.
Sam Have you ever ⁵_____ down Mount Everest?
Gordon No, I haven't. But I ⁶_____ down Mont Blanc in 1977!
Pam Have you ⁷_____ any films?
Gordon Yes, I ⁸_____ a film about Tibet in 1957.

b Write four sentences about things you have done.
When did you do these things?

I've eaten Indian food. I ate a curry last F

4 **I can use the present perfect to talk about recent news.**

   a Can you remember Phoebe's news? Use the pictures to help you.

She's just changed her hairstyle

1 She _____ her hairstyle.

2 Bonny _____ three kittens.

3 Oscar _____ an MP3 player.

4 Her mum and dad _____ the kitchen.

5 Her dad _____ his back.

6 Her mum _____ a new job at a vet's.

   b Write three pieces of news about yourself.

I've just ...

5 **I know how to use verbs and nouns together correctly.**

Match the verbs in A to the nouns in B to make phrases.

A		B
1 break	**a**	a bike
2 travel	**b**	a mountain
3 climb	**c**	in a river
4 make	**d**	a ball
5 swim	**e**	on a train
6 throw	**f**	a leg
7 ride	**g**	a cake

Extra special

What's just happened?

a Work in a small team. Look at the picture. Find the twelve people who have just done these things. The first team to write the 12 correct letters is the winner.

1 j

1 He has just thrown a ball.
2 He has just scored a goal.
3 She has just jumped into the water.
4 He has just hurt his leg.
5 She has just bought an ice cream.
6 She has just fallen off her bike.
7 He has just got out of the pool.
8 He has just come into the park.
9 She has just dropped the ball.
10 He has just sat down.
11 She has just dived into the water.
12 She has just taken a photo.

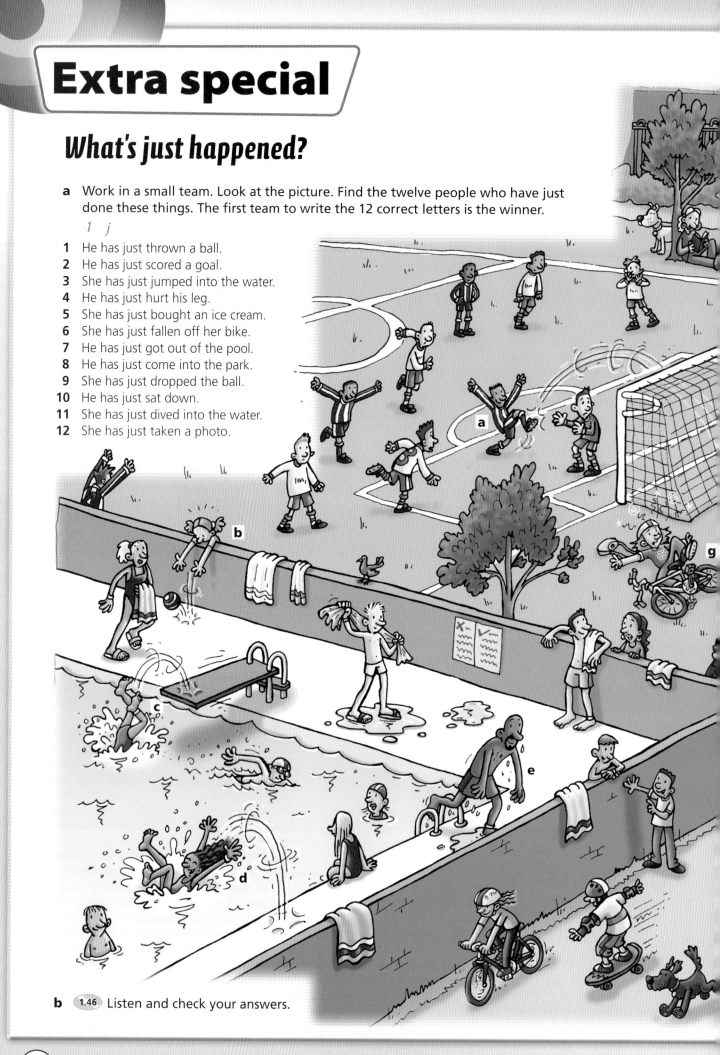

b (1.46) Listen and check your answers.

Mini-project

1 Read Helen's poster. Have you done anything similar?

My latest news ...

These are some things I've done:

1 I've played netball for my school team. We won 11–6.

2 I've just passed my Maths test. I got a very good mark!

3 I've made some biscuits. They were delicious!

4 I've just started piano lessons. I had my first lesson last week.

5 I've been to the dentist. I went yesterday.

Helen

2 Make a poster about your news. Write at least five sentences.

3 Show your poster to your classmates. Answer questions about your news.

13 The talent show

1 Vocabulary

2.01 Find these words in the picture.

costume d

> costume   judge
> microphone
> audience
> stage   guitar

16th February @ 2pm

The School Talent Show

★ Sing! ★
Act! ★
Dance! ★
Entertain! ★ ★

1st prize: **Gold medal**

2nd prize: **Silver medal**

3rd prize: **Bronze medal**

2 Presentation

2.02 Listen and read Phoebe's and Oscar's diaries. What do they think will happen at the talent show?

15th February

It's the School talent show tomorrow and I'm dreading it. Will I remember the words to my song? Will the audience fall asleep? I think it'll be a disaster. I'll fall off the stage and I'll drop my guitar. The microphone won't work and my friends will laugh at me.

15th February

I can't wait for the show tomorrow! I think it'll be great! I'll dance brilliantly and I won't make any mistakes. My costume will look amazing. My friends will all cheer for me.

The judges will love me and I'll win the first prize. Then my picture will be in the local newspaper and I'll be famous.

3 Comprehension

What are Oscar and Phoebe's predictions?
Read again then answer the questions.

1 The microphone.

1 What won't work?
2 Who will fall off the stage?
3 Who will have an amazing costume?
4 Who won't make any mistakes?
5 Who will laugh at Oscar?
6 Who will love Phoebe?

Real English

I can't wait for …
I'm dreading it.

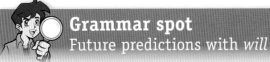

Grammar spot
Future predictions with *will*

I**'ll** fall off the stage.
My friends **will** laugh at me.
I **won't** make any mistakes.
Will I remember the words to the song?
Yes, I **will**./No, I **won't**.

📖 Grammar page 102

❹ Grammar practice

a Phoebe and Oscar are talking about the talent show. Use *will*, *'ll* or *won't* to complete the dialogue.

1 it'll be
2 won't remember

Oscar Oh Phoebe, I'm really worried about the talent show. I'm sure it ¹_____ (be) a disaster. I ²_____ (not remember) the words to my song and the judges ³_____ (hate) me.

Phoebe Don't be silly, Oscar! You ⁴_____ (sing) really well and you ⁵_____ (play) your guitar brilliantly. You ⁶_____ (not forget) the words to your song, and the judges ⁷_____ (give) you the silver medal.

Oscar The silver medal! Who ⁸_____ (get) the gold medal?

Phoebe I will, of course!

b 🔊 2.03 Listen and check your answers.

❺ Speaking

a Write three predictions about your future. Use the ideas in the box.

I think I'll be a teacher. I'll travel to another country and I'll speak six languages.

> be a pop star
> be a pilot
> be a teacher
> live in a big house
> marry a famous person
> have ten children
> meet an important stranger
> travel to another country
> win an amazing prize
> speak six languages
> help other people
> design an amazing invention

b Work in pairs. Can you guess your partner's predictions?

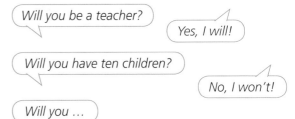

Will you be a teacher?

Yes, I will!

Will you have ten children?

No, I won't!

Will you …

My English file

Write four true predictions about your future. Use your own ideas.

I think I will learn to drive a train and …

❻ Check your English

Choose the correct verb from the box with *will* or *won't* to complete these predictions.

> become   cheer   not forget
> dance   give   not fall over

1 Phoebe _____ well at the Talent Show.
2 The judges _____ Phoebe a gold medal.
3 Phoebe _____ a famous dancer.
4 Oscar _____ at the Talent Show.
5 He _____ the words to his song.
6 The audience _____ loudly.

14 Helpful Herbert

❶ Vocabulary

2.04 Look at the pictures and find these words.

violin   d

violin   drums   keyboards   recorder
double bass   accordion   flute   amp

❷ Presentation

2.05 Listen and read. Who asks Herbert to:

1 close the window?
2 get some food?
3 fix the amp?

Oh, I'm so cold. Herbert, could you close the window, please. And can I borrow your scarf?

Yes, of course. And I'll find some gloves for you.

Vicky

Art

Bob

Gabby

Herbert

Dan

1

2

Herbert, I'm really hungry. Can you get a sandwich for me?

And could you buy some crisps for me?

Sure. I'll get some drinks, too.

3

Ooops!

Oh dear!

4

The amp doesn't work, Herbert. Could you fix it?

No problem, Dan. And I'll turn up the volume as well.

VOLUME

5

6

7

Real English

Sure.
No problem.
Oh, dear.
Of course.

44

❸ Comprehension

Read the story again. What three things does Herbert offer to do?

1 find some gloves for Gabby

Grammar spot
Requests and offers

Requests: *can*/*could*
Can I borrow your scarf, please?
Can you get a sandwich for me?
Could you close the window, please?

Offers
I'll find some gloves for you.
I'll get some drinks.

👀 **Grammar page 102**

❹ Grammar practice

a Put the words in order to make requests.

1 I'm hot. Could you open the window, please?

1 I'm hot.

| open | Could | the window | please | you | ? |

2 I'm thirsty.

| a drink | you | Could | for | me | get |
| please | ? |

3 I'm bored.

| please | your magazine | I | Could | borrow | ? |

4 I can't find the library.

| Could | please | I | your map | look at | ? |

5 My head hurts.

| you | Could | please | quiet | be | ? |

b Now make offers from these prompts.

1 I'll buy an ice cream for you.

1 I/buy/an ice cream for you.
2 I/make/a cup of tea for you.
3 I/switch on/the TV.
4 I/walk there/with you.
5 I/get/some medicine for you.

Study tip

Record verbs and nouns that go together.

open + window   switch on + TV

❺ Listening

a **2.06** Listen to these four people. What are the problems? Complete the sentences.

I want to go to the _____, but my _____ is broken.

I can't find my _____.

I want to phone my _____, but I haven't got a _____.

I don't _____ the _____.

b Think of an offer for each problem.

I'll lend you my bike.

❻ Pronunciation

2.07 Listen and practise saying these requests. Notice the intonation.

1 Could you fix my computer?
2 Can I borrow your calculator?
3 Could I look at your book?
4 Could you fetch my coat?
5 Can you close the door?
6 Can I use your MP3 player?

❼ Check your English

a Choose the correct words and make requests.

1 Could *I/you* open the door for me, please?
2 Can *I/you* use your phone, please?
3 Could *I/you* borrow your DVD, please?
4 Could *I/you* switch on the light for me, please?

b Put these words into the correct order to make offers.

1 | your | for | fix | bike | you | I'll |

2 | you | snack | I'll | a | get | for |

3 | some | I'll | lend | money | you |

15 The festival

❶ Presentation

(2.08) Listen. Mel, Sophie and Charlie are at the Edinburgh Festival with Sophie's dad. What do they want to see? Complete the speech bubbles.

I want to see the New York Street Dancers.

How about going to this _____.

I want to see _____.

Let's listen to _____.

Saturday afternoon, 25th August at the Edinburgh Festival.	
Venue	**Show**
Queen's Hall	Shakespeare's classic play: Romeo & Juliet
The Music Box	River Roots Band: modern folk music
New Theatre	Puppet Show: Sleeping Beauty
The Assembly Rooms	Comedy Show
Festival Tent	Peppo's Circus
The Bongo Club	The New York Street Dancers
Cabaret Club	The Modern Mime Men

❷ Comprehension

(2.08) Listen again. Are these sentences true or false?

1 Mel saw the New York Street Dancers on TV last year.
2 Charlie says dance is boring.
3 The River Roots Band is Mel's favourite band.
4 Charlie hates folk music.
5 Mel, Charlie and Sophie think that Sophie's dad's decision is a good idea.

Real English

No way!
It's so lame!
They're wicked!

❸ Vocabulary

Match the word in A to its definition in B.

1 c

	A		B
1	mime	**a**	a doll with strings
2	comedy	**b**	traditional music from a country
3	circus	**c**	acting with no talking
4	puppet	**d**	a travelling group of performers
5	folk music	**e**	a funny play or film

❹ Grammar practice

a Use the correct form of the verb in brackets to complete this conversation.

1 to go

Grammar spot
Making and responding to suggestions

How about going to this show?
Let's listen to the River Roots Band.
Would you like to see the comedy show?

I'd like to see this Shakespeare play.
I **don't want to** see dance.
No way.
Good idea.

🎧 Grammar page 103

Saturday night, 25th August at the Edinburgh Festival.

Venue	Show
Edinburgh Castle	Fireworks
Cabaret club	Mime and Modern Dance
New Theatre	Puppet Show: Robin Hood
Ross Open Air Theatre	Mozart's classic opera: The Magic Flute
Festival Tent	Peppo's Circus
The Bongo Club	Comedy Club Night
The Music Box	Jazz and Blues Band

Dad Would you like ¹ _____ (go) to the festival tonight?
Charlie Let's ² _____ (walk) to the Castle and ³ _____ (watch) the fireworks.
Mel No, I don't like fireworks.
Sophie How about ⁴ _____ (go) to the Opera in the Park?
Charlie Oh no! Boring!
Dad Let's ⁵ _____ (go) back to the hotel and ⁶ _____ (watch) TV.
Mel, Sophie, Charlie No way!

b (2.09) Listen and check.

❺ Speaking

a Work with two or three classmates. Design your own festival programme.

b Exchange programmes with another group. Choose a show. Make suggestions and reach a group decision.

What would you like to see, Mika?

How about …

❻ Check your English

Put these sentences into the correct order.

1 What would you like to do tonight?

1 you · what · to · tonight · would · do · like · ?

2 about · cinema · going · how · to · the · ?

3 don't · watch · I · a · to · film · want

4 listen · the · band · let's · to · jazz

5 walk · you · would · to · park · the
afternoon · like · to · this · ?

16 The Brit School

❶ Reading

a (2.10) Read the article. What do students learn at the Brit School?

The Brit School

Would you like to learn how to dance?

How about learning to play the drums?

Lunch break has just started at The Brit School, in South East London, and there's an hour before lessons begin again. However, at this school, the students want to study during their lunch break. Outside, three students are playing the guitar together and are writing a song. In the corridor inside, another student is stretching and practising some dance exercises. And in the library, some friends are doing their homework and talking about their dreams and plans for the future. Freya thinks that she will be a singer and star in famous musicals in the West End of London. Bill thinks he'll be a soap star and Tania hopes she'll be a successful actress.

The Brit School is a special performing arts school for 14-19 year olds who want to work in music, theatre, dance or design. The school is state-funded. This means that the students don't pay any money to go to the school. The students have to work very hard at The Brit School. 'People think that we have a lot of fun here and sing and dance all day,' says 16-year-old Tania, 'but there are a lot of things to learn. We also study the normal school subjects: History, Science, English, Maths and IT. By Friday afternoon, I'm always exhausted!'

The Brit School opened in 1991 and it now has some very famous old students. Adele, Katie Melua, The Kooks and Athlete, all went to The Brit School.

b Find these words in the article. Can you guess what they mean?

> corridor   stretching   musicals
> successful   state-funded   exhausted

c Read the article again and answer the questions.

1 Where is The Brit School?
2 How long is the lunch break?
3 How old are the students at the school?
4 What subjects do students study?
5 When did the school open?

❷ Listening

a (2.11) Tim wants to go to the Brit School. Listen to his interview. What does he want to study at the Brit School?

b (2.11) Listen again and complete the dialogue.

Teacher	So, Tim, why do you want to come to this school?
Tim	Well, I really love ¹_____ and I think that this school is a great place to learn. I want to study ²_____ here.
Teacher	Hmm. I see. What job do you think you'll have in the future?
Tim	I hope I'll ³_____ a professional singer. I think I'll be in a band and we'll ⁴_____ and ⁵_____ our own songs.
Teacher	Do you ⁶_____ your music at home?
Tim	Yes, I do. I sing every day, even in the holidays. And I'm also ⁷_____ to play the guitar.
Teacher	Who is your favourite singer?
Tim	I really love Justin Timberlake. I think he's got an amazing voice and he's a great ⁸_____ too.

❸ Speaking

Act out the interview. Work in pairs.

Student A: You are a teacher at the Brit School. Student B wants to join your school. Ask the questions below. Think of two more questions for Student B.

Student B: You want to go to the Brit School. Prepare your answers to the questions below.

- What do you want to study at the school?
- What job do you think you'll have in the future?
- Do you practise at home?
- Who is your favourite singer/actor/dancer?

So Michelle, what do you want to study at the school?

I want to study dancing …

❹ Writing

Write a paragraph to explain why you want to go to the Brit School. Use your ideas from Activity 3.

I want to go to the Brit School because I really like …

Writing tip

Use different ways of writing about what you like and what you want:

I **really like** theatre and dance.
I **really love** singing.
I **want to** study music.
I **hope** I'll be a professional singer.
I **enjoy** acting.
I **think** I'll be an actress.

Let's go swimming

Work in groups of three or four.

Student A: Make a suggestion about what to do today. Use *Let's go.*

Student B: Repeat Student A's suggestion and add your own idea.

Student C: Repeat Student A's and B's suggestions and add your own idea.

If you forget a suggestion, you're out of the game.

Let's go swimming today.

Let's go swimming and play football today.

Let's go swimming, play football and watch a DVD today.

Review

Check you can do these things.

1 I can make predictions about the future with *will*.

a Write Oscar's and Phoebe's predictions about the School Talent Show.

1 I will drop my guitar.

1 I/drop my guitar
2 the microphone/not work
3 my friends/laugh at me

4 I/dance really well
5 I/not make any mistakes
6 my/costume/look amazing

b Make questions. Then ask and answer with a classmate.

Will you get married?

1 get married?
2 live in another country?
3 be famous?
4 be rich?
5 be happy?

No, I won't!

2 I know the names of six instruments.

Write the correct words next to the instrument.

1 v _ _ _ _ _

2 d _ _ _ _

3 k _ _ _ _ _ _ _ _

4 d _ _ _ _ _   b _ _ _

5 a _ _ _ _ _ _ _ _

6 f _ _ _ _

3 I can make requests with *could* and *can*.

Complete the request for each picture. Use the words in the box.

> borrow your dictionary   give me a drink   open the window
> listen to your MP3 player   close the door   fix my camera

1 Could you open the window?

1 Could you _____?

3 Can I _____?

5 Can I _____?

2 Could you _____?

4 Could I _____?

6 Could you _____?

4 I can make offers with *will*.

Read about these problems. Make an offer for each problem with *I'll*.

1 I'll help you look for it.

1 I can't find my bag.
2 I don't understand my homework.
3 My phone is broken.
4 I'm very cold.
5 This suitcase is very heavy.
6 I'm very hungry.

5 I can make suggestions with *Let's* and *How about*.

Complete these suggestions with *Let's* or *How about*.

1 _____ go to the cinema tonight.
2 _____ watch the football match on TV.
3 _____ listening to some music?
4 _____ play a computer game.
5 _____ taking the dog for a walk?

6 I know the names of different types of entertainment.

Look at the pictures and complete the crossword.

1

2

4

3

5

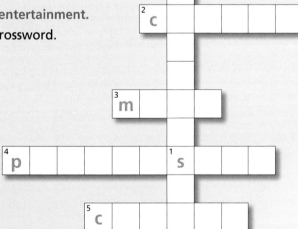

> **Extra reading**
> Turn to page 94 and read an extract from *The Adventures of Tom Sawyer*.

Extra special

In the year 2030

Answer the questions about yourself. Find out what your future will be!

1 What's your favourite sport?

a swimming
b chess
c horse riding

2 Your friend is bored. What do you say?

a Let's go to the beach.
b How about playing a computer game?
c Let's take the dog for a walk.

3 Your brother/sister wants to get a pet. What do you say?

a How about getting a fish?
b No way! I don't like pets.
c Good idea! Let's get a dog, two cats, a rabbit and a hamster.

4 What's your favourite animal?

a a dolphin
b a computer mouse
c a tiger

5 You go shopping with your mum and dad. What do you buy?

a a swimming costume
b a CD
c a book about animals

6 Your mum and dad are planning a day trip. Where do you want to go?

a The Aquarium
b The Science Museum
c The Zoo

7 Who's your favourite cartoon character?

a Spongebob Squarepants
b WALL-E
c Scooby Doo

8 What posters have you got on your bedroom wall?

a pictures of fish, dolphins and whales
b pictures of space rockets and gadgets
c pictures of lions, tigers and elephants

Score

Mostly a's

In the year 2030, you will be a professional diver. You will go on beach holidays every summer and in the winter you will live in a submarine. You won't be rich or famous but you will be very happy. Your best friend will be a dolphin.

Mostly b's

In the year 2030, you will be a computer expert. You will travel around the world in your own high-speed jet. You will invent amazing new computers and you will be very rich. Your best friend will be a robot.

Mostly c's

In the year 2030, you will be a zookeeper. You will learn to communicate with animals and you will appear on your own television programme called 'The Animal Expert'. You won't be very rich but you will be very famous. Your best friend will be a chimpanzee.

Mini-project

1 Look at Joanne's FactFile about the Glastonbury Festival.

festival factfile

- The Glastonbury festival is the biggest open-air music and performing arts festival in the world.
- There are more than 70 different stages and over 700 different acts.
- It started in 1970 but it became popular in the 1980s.
- It usually happens at the end of June and it lasts for three days.
- More than 150,000 people now go to the Glastonbury festival.

Joanne

2 Find out about an important festival in your country.

- When did it start?
- When does it happen?
- What kind of festival is it?
- How many people usually go to it?

Use pictures from magazines or draw pictures to illustrate your Festival FactFile.

Lesson objectives
● Talking about illness
● Talking about future possibilities

17 How are you feeling?

❶ Vocabulary

2.12 Listen. Match the words with the pictures.

> flu   medicine   a temperature   a sore throat
> a cold   a headache   a cough   a stomach ache

flu e

 a **b** **c** **d** **e** **f** **g** **h**

❷ Presentation

a 2.13 Listen and read. Does Phoebe think Oscar is really ill?

Phoebe	Hello Oscar. How are you feeling?
Oscar	Terrible. I'm really ill. I've got a headache and I've got a sore throat. And I've got a cough.
Phoebe	Umm. Have you been to the doctor?
Oscar	Yes, I have. I think I've got flu.
Phoebe	Have you got a temperature?
Oscar	Yes, I think so.
Phoebe	Let's see. Umm. No, you haven't. Your temperature's normal. I think you've only got a cold.
Oscar	But I feel terrible.
Phoebe	Have you taken your medicine?
Oscar	No, I haven't.
Phoebe	Well, if you don't take your medicine, you won't get better.
Oscar	But it tastes horrible.
Phoebe	Go on. Take it. And what are you doing? If you watch TV, your headache will get worse. Give me the remote.
Oscar	But I was watching that!
Phoebe	And I think I'll take this chocolate away …
Oscar	But …
Phoebe	If you eat all this chocolate, you'll get a stomach ache. And if you get a stomach ache, you'll have to stay at home another day. And I know you don't want to miss school again, Oscar!

b 2.13 Listen again. Which of the health problems from Activity 1 does Oscar say he has?

Real English

How are you feeling?
I feel terrible.
Go on.

Grammar spot
First conditional

If you **watch** TV, your headache **will get** worse.
If you **don't take** your medicine, you **won't get** better.

👀 **Grammar page 103**

Writing tip
comma

If you watch TV, your headache will get worse.

❸ Grammar practice

Match the words in A with the words in B to make sentences.

A
1 If you study hard,
2 If you don't go to bed now,
3 If you eat lots of apples,
4 If you don't get up now,
5 If you don't write notes,

B
a you'll get a stomach ache.
b you'll be late for school.
c you won't remember the answers.
d you'll pass the test.
e you'll feel tired in the morning.

❹ Pronunciation

a (2.14) Listen to this tongue twister.

/t/

Take Tony's temperature tonight and tomorrow.

b (2.15) Listen again and repeat. How fast can you say it?

❺ Speaking

a Complete these sentences with your own ideas.

1 If my friend is late, I won't wait for him.

1 If my friend is late, I'll/I won't …
2 If it rains tomorrow, I'll/I won't …
3 If you watch too much TV, you'll …
4 If …, I'll watch TV.
5 If it …, I won't go to the beach.
6 If you eat all that ice-cream, you'll …

b Now work with a classmate.
Student A: Say the first part of the sentence.
Student B: Finish the sentence. Then swap roles.

If my friend is late,

I won't wait for him.

❻ Check your English

a Find eight words connected to health in this word puzzle.

D	I	M	C	O	U	G	H	K	F	P	V	M	E
S	R	R	Y	I	T	S	E	Q	L	J	E	S	R
K	T	E	M	P	E	R	A	T	U	R	E	T	W
B	S	T	J	C	W	A	D	G	C	S	A	N	O
H	R	A	S	T	O	M	A	C	H	A	C	H	E
E	U	Q	H	B	U	U	C	V	L	Y	O	L	R
G	W	D	B	X	M	M	H	Z	H	I	L	U	E
M	E	D	I	C	I	N	E	P	O	E	D	Y	K
M	R	O	S	O	R	E	T	H	R	O	A	T	C

b Answer these questions.

1 Is your temperature normal?
2 How many of these things have you had?
   a flu
   b a sore throat
   c a cough
3 Have you got any of them now?
4 Have you been to the doctor this year?
5 Do you think these sentences are true?
   a If you watch a lot of TV, you'll get a headache.
   b If you eat a lot of chocolate, you'll get a stomach ache.
6 Do you stay away from school when you are ill?

18 I'm worried

❶ Vocabulary

2.16 Find these things in the pictures.

games   insect spray   torch
bull   tent   warm clothes

❷ Presentation

a 2.17 Listen and read. What do you think Nicole and her friends are doing this weekend?

Sophie I'm worried it may be cold.
Nicole Don't worry. It may not be cold, but if it is, we'll wear warm clothes.
Sophie Oh, yes, good idea.
Mel I'm worried there may be a lot of insects.
Nicole Don't worry. I'm going to take some insect spray. If there are lots of insects, we'll spray them.
Mel Ah, yes, of course.
Sophie I'm also worried it may rain all the time.
Nicole Don't worry. If it rains all the time, we'll play games in the tent.
Sophie Yes, that's a great idea.
Nicole Anyway the weather's going to be great this weekend. We can go for a walk in the countryside.
Mel But we may see some bulls.
Sophie Yes, there may be bulls.
Nicole Umm. Yes, well, if we see any bulls … we'll run!

b 2.17 Listen again. What four things are Sophie and Mel worried about? Choose from the box. Then read the dialogue with your classmates.

bulls   games   insect spray   the tent   rain
insects   clothes   cold   the countryside

Grammar spot
may (possibility)

It **may be** cold.
It **may not be** cold.
There **may be** a lot of insects.
We **may see** some bulls.

👓 Grammar page 103

❸ Grammar practice

2.18 Sophie and Mel have some more worries. Listen then complete the dialogue with these words:

> lost   dark   hot   hungry

> make some sandwiches   switch on the torch   look at our map   go for a swim

1

| **Mel** | It may be very _____. |
| **Nicole** | If it's very _____, we'll _____. |

2

| **Mel** | We may be _____. |
| **Nicole** | If we are _____, we'll _____. |

3

| **Sophie** | We may get _____. |
| **Nicole** | If we're _____, we'll _____. |

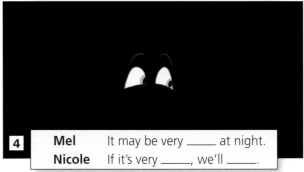

4

| **Mel** | It may be very _____ at night. |
| **Nicole** | If it's very _____, we'll _____. |

❹ Speaking

a Make lists of the things you are *going to do* and the things you *may do* this weekend. Don't show your classmates.

Things I'm going to do	*Things I may do*
hang out with my friends	*play football*
go shopping	*buy some new*
jeans	

b Now ask your classmates about their plans for this weekend.

> What are you going to do this weekend?

> I'm going to hang out with my friends. We may play football. What are you going to do?

> I'm going to …

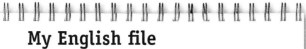

My English file

Think about your plans for the next school holiday. Write about the things you are *going to do* and the things you *may do*.

My next school holiday

In my next school holiday I'm going to go camping with my family. We may go to the mountains or we may go to the beach. I'm also going to …

❺ Check your English

a Choose the sentence that is true about you this weekend.

1
a   I'm going to hang out with my friends.
b   I may hang out with my friends.
c   I'm not going to hang out with my friends.

2
a   I'm going to tidy my room.
b   I may tidy my room.
c   I'm not going to tidy my room.

b Nicole is thinking about this weekend. Complete with:

> be   go   play   meet   is   rains   watch

> If it ¹_____, I'll ²_____ games or ³_____ TV. But it may ⁴_____ hot. If it ⁵_____ hot, I'll ⁶_____ my friends and ⁷_____ swimming.

19 You should say thank you

❶ Guessing

Look at the pictures. Rachel, Sun and Lukas are talking about customs where they live. Can you guess what customs they are talking about?

❷ Presentation

a `2.19` Listen and read. Check your ideas.

1 Amish people look different, but you shouldn't stare at us. We think it's rude. We like visitors, but you shouldn't come on Sundays because we go to church and spend time with our family then.

2 When someone gives you a present, you should say thank you. But you shouldn't open the present immediately. People think that's very rude. You can open the present when you get home.

3 Where I live, you shouldn't wear your shoes inside someone's house. There's a lot of snow in the Yukon in the winter and people don't want wet shoes in their homes. Even in the summer it is often muddy and dirty so you should always take off your shoes.

b `2.19` Listen and read again. Have you got the same customs where you live?

Grammar spot
obligation and advice
should, shouldn't

You **should say** thank you.
You **shouldn't stare** at us.

Grammar page 104

❸ Grammar practice

a Look at the sentences. Can you guess what the missing word is: *should* or *shouldn't?*

Customs around the world

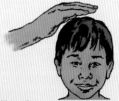

1 In Thailand …
You _____ pat anyone on the top of the head.

2 In the UK …
You _____ say, 'Bless you' when someone sneezes.

3 In Saudi Arabia …
You _____ say no to coffee when you visit someone's home.

4 In China …
You _____ leave some food on your plate when you eat at someone's house.

b 〔2.20〕 Listen and check. Do you have the same customs in your country?

❹ Class poll

a Brainstorm some customs where you live and write them on the board. Here are some ideas:

> meals   birthdays   weddings   presents   school   buses

b Now vote for the custom you think is most important.

> You shouldn't talk with your mouth full of food.
>
> You should stand up when the teacher comes in the room.

❺ Speaking

a Match the problems in A with the advice in B.

> *I've got hiccups.*
>
> *You should drink lots of water.*

A   **B**

1 I've got hiccups.   **a** You should count sheep.

2 I can't sleep at night.   **b** You shouldn't eat cheese at night.

3 I've got flu.   **c** You should drink lots of water.

4 I have bad dreams.   **d** You shouldn't sleep on your back.

5 I snore when I sleep.   **e** You should stay in bed.

b Can you give some different advice for the problems?

❻ Song

〔2.21〕 Find the song *I Have a Dream* on page 90.

❼ Check your English

Write mini dialogues about three of these problems using *should/shouldn't.*

> I'm cold.   I'm hungry.   I'm not fit.
> I've got a headache.   I'm sad.
> I've hurt my leg.   I'm tired.
> I've got a stomach ache.
> I'm thirsty.   I've lost my bag.

> A: I'm cold.
> B: You should wear warm clothes.

20 Survival

1 Reading

a (2.22) Read the questionnaire. Use a dictionary to help with words you don't understand.

What should you do?

You are walking in a forest in Canada. You turn a corner and see a black bear in front of you. The bear begins to walk towards you. What should you do?

    A Speak to the bear in a very quiet voice.
    B Run away.
    C Climb a tree.

You are lost in a jungle and are trying to find a village or a town. You are very tired and hungry. You find a river. What should you do?

    A Walk along the river upstream.
    B Go back into the jungle.
    C Walk along the river downstream.

Your car has got a puncture. You are in the middle of a forest and you can't see any houses. There is a terrible storm and you are worried lightning will hit your car. What should you do?

    A Climb under the car.
    B Stand under a tree.
    C Stay in the car.

You are in your room and you see there is a fire in your bin. There is a window but your bedroom is on the third floor. There is a lot of smoke and flames and the door is on the other side of the room. What should you do?

    A Open the window and shout for help.
    B Crawl along the floor to the door.
    C Run to the door.

b Read again. Work in a small team. Agree on one answer and write it down.

c (2.23) Listen and check.

❷ Speaking

Can you remember? Work with a classmate. Ask and answer about the situations in Activity 1.

You see a bear. What should you do?   *You should …*

❸ Listening

2.24 Look at pictures 1 and 2 in Activity 1 and listen. Then write the missing words.

a ¹speak

> run walk climbers dangerous
> running climb speak run tree

a You should ¹_____ to the bear in a very quiet voice and then ²_____ away. This is still ³_____ but it is better than ⁴_____ away. If you ⁵_____, bears will nearly always ⁶_____ after you. You also shouldn't ⁷_____ a ⁸_____ because bears are very good ⁹_____.

> downstream village walk river
> jungle closer go back upstream

b You should ¹_____ along the river ²_____. This is better than walking ³_____. You have got a better chance of finding a ⁴_____ or town on lower land ⁵_____ to the sea. You shouldn't ⁶_____ into the ⁷_____ as you may not find the ⁸_____ again.

❹ Writing

Work with a classmate. Write your own survival situation. Use the situations in Activity 1 as a model. Use a dictionary to help with new vocabulary.

> You are swimming in the sea and see a shark. The shark is very close to you and is opening its mouth. What should you do?
>
> A Swim away from the shark.
> B Shout for help.
> C Hit the shark in the eye.

Observation game

a **2.25** Look at the picture and listen. Try to find the people. Don't tell your classmates the answers.

b **2.25** Now work in a small team. Listen again. Match the people with the sentences you hear. Write your answers. The first team with all the correct answers is the winner.

Review

Check you can do these things.

1 I know words about illness.
Unscramble these words.

1 d c m e e i n i   **2** r o s e   r a t t o h   **3** g u c o h   **4** r t u r e e t m e a p

5 l d c o   **6** c h m o s t a   h e a c   **7** d a c e e a h h   **8** l u f

2 I can talk about future possibilities.
Complete these sentences with the correct form of the verbs in brackets.

1 If you _____ (eat) all that chocolate, you _____ (get) a stomach ache.
2 If you _____ (take) this medicine, you _____ (feel) better.
3 If you _____ (not/hurry) up, we _____ (miss) the bus.
4 If you _____ (drop) the pot, you _____ (break) it.
5 If I _____ (go) out in the rain without a coat, I _____ (catch) a cold.

3 I can talk about possible events.

a Can you remember what Sophie and Mel worried about?
Use the phrases in brackets and *may*.

1 It may rain.

1 It _____ (rain).
2 We _____ (be cold).
3 There _____ (be a lot of insects).
4 We _____ (see some bulls).

b What are Nicole's good ideas?
Use the prompts to write Nicole's ideas.

1 If/rain/play games in our tent.
2 If/cold/wear warm clothes.
3 If/a lot of insects/spray them.
4 If/see some bulls/run!

4 I can describe plans for the future.

Look at Toby's list of plans for next week and write sentences with *may* or *going to*. The plans with ✓ are definite plans. The plans with ? are possible plans.

1 He's going to play football next week.

2 He may go to the library next week.

Plans for next week
1 play football ✓
2 go to library ?
3 visit my cousins ?
4 start on my school project ✓
5 send an email to Ben ?
6 clean my bike ✓
7 tidy my room ?
8 go swimming ?
9 watch TV ✓
10 buy a new CD ✓

5 I can give advice with *should* and *shouldn't*.

a Read the problems. Use the words in brackets to give advice with *you should* or *you shouldn't*.

1 You should wear a warm coat.

1 It's very cold outside.
(wear/warm coat)

2 I've got a stomach ache.
(eat/a lot of sweets)

3 I'm on the beach and it's very hot.
(put on/suncream)

4 I'm very tired.
(go to bed/late)

6 I know about customs in different countries.

Make sentences about what you *should* and *shouldn't* do in these countries. Use the ideas in the box.

say 'no' to coffee when you visit someone's home
pat anyone on the top of the head
leave some food on your plate when you eat at someone's house
say 'Bless you' when someone sneezes

1 In Thailand …
2 In the UK …
3 In Saudi Arabia …
4 In China …

Extra special

Round the world jigsaw

a Work with two or three classmates. Match the puzzle pieces to make sentences. Use the pictures to help you.

Tip

Don't worry if you don't know one of the answers. Do the easiest ones first and then guess the difficult ones!

INDIA

2 If you go to India, you may …

USA

1 If you go to the USA, you may …

a pick tulips.

ICELAND

5 If you go to Iceland, you may …

Paris

FRANCE

6 If you go to Paris, you may …

EGYPT

3 If you go to Egypt, you may …

UK

London

4 If you go to London, you may …

SCOTLAND

7 If you go to Scotland, you may …

AUSTRALIA

8 If you go to Australia, you may …

g see Big Ben.

Netherlands

9 If you go to the Netherlands, you may …

Venice

ITALY

10 If you go to Venice, you may …

i ride a camel.

b take a photo of kangaroos.

c see the volcano Mount Helka.

d see the Eiffel Tower.

e see men wearing kilts.

f ride in a gondola.

h visit the Taj Mahal.

j visit the Grand Canyon.

b Read your sentences. Compare your ideas with your classmates.

c (2.26) Listen and check your answers. You get 1 point for every correct guess.

Mini-project

1 Read Nathan's poster. What is Nathan's best piece of advice?

How to keep fit
Six pieces of advice

1

You should do ten minutes of exercise every morning.

2
You shouldn't take the bus to school. You should walk or cycle.

3

You should eat lots of fruit and vegetables.

4
You shouldn't eat lots of sweets or chocolate.

5 You should go for a run every day.

6

You shouldn't take lifts. You should walk up the stairs.

Nathan

2 Make a poster with some 'How to' advice. Here are some ideas:

How to pass tests
How to wake up early
How to keep your room tidy
How to make friends
How to become a star student

3 Compare your poster with your classmates. Do you agree with their advice?

21 DIY disasters

❶ Vocabulary

2.27 Find these things in the picture.

hammer   ladder   window   toolbox   paint   drill   wallpaper

hammer   c

❷ Presentation

a Match the names in A with the phrases in B to make sentences about what you think is going to happen.

1 Helga is going to spill the paint.

	A		B
1	Helga	**a**	is going to eat Mandy's cake.
2	Martha	**b**	are going to break the window.
3	Rudolph	**c**	is going to spill the paint.
4	Vincent	**d**	is going to fall off the ladder.
5	Pam and Sam	**e**	is going to drop the toolbox.
6	Bonehead	**f**	is going to trip over the drill.

b **2.28** Listen to the Glooms and check your answers.

Study tip
Verbs + prepositions

Record verbs with their prepositions.

trip **over**   fall **off**

❸ Grammar practice

a Look at these pictures and make predictions with *going to*.

1 He's going to fall off the chair.

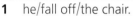

Grammar page 104

Grammar spot
Future predictions with *going to*

She**'s going to** spill the paint.
They**'re going to** break the window.

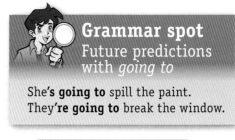

1 he/fall off/the chair. **2** she/spill/her cereal.

3 they/trip over/the ladder. **4** he/drop/the books. **5** the ball/break/the window.

b (2.29) Listen and check.

❹ Writing

Look at the picture and make predictions about what is *going to* happen.

| break | spill | drop | eat | fall off | trip over |

| the tins | the chair | the broom |
| the glass | the biscuits | the water |

1 Vincent is going to spill the water.

1 Vincent _____. **4** Rudolph _____.
2 Martha _____. **5** Mandy _____.
3 Sam and Pam _____. **6** Bonehead _____.

❺ Game

Pretend you are *going to* do something. Choose one of the ideas below. Mime it to your friends. Can they guess what you are *going to* do?

fall off a chair	drop a plate
fall asleep	eat some soup
sneeze	go swimming
drink a glass of water	run in a race

You're going to drop a plate! *No, I'm not.*

You're going to fall off a chair! *Yes, I am.*

❻ Check your English

Match the phrases in A with the phrases in B to make sentences.

A
1 Look! The apples
2 Look at the clouds. It
3 Jack has got tennis racket and a tennis ball. He
4 Helen is shouting very loudly. She

B
a 's going to play tennis.
b 's going to wake the baby.
c 's going to rain.
d are going to fall off the tree.

22 My home

1 Presentation

a (2.30) Listen and read. Match the pictures to the texts.

What is your home like?

1 I don't get many visitors to my house and it's very peaceful here. That's because I live in an old **lighthouse**! Sometimes it's very quiet and not exciting enough, but I've got a beautiful view of the sea. There's another problem – there are too many stairs in my house!!

2 I live in a **caravan** with my mum and dad. It hasn't got many rooms and I sleep on a sofa in the living room. Some people think our caravan is very small, but it's big enough for us. We've got enough **furniture**: a TV, a sofa, a table and three chairs. And I've got some books and DVDs, so I'm happy. We can travel around and meet different people in different places.

3 I live in the outback of Australia on a big **ranch**. I don't go to school; it's 200 kilometres away. But I have some online lessons every day and I talk to my teacher on the radio. I like living on a ranch but there aren't enough people here, so sometimes I get a bit lonely.

4 I live in a pretty **cottage** in a village. In the summer a lot of tourists visit this village and there's too much **traffic** and noise. I don't like it then because it's very busy and it's not quiet enough. But in the winter there aren't many people here and it's quiet and beautiful.

b Which do you think is the best place to live? Which place is the worst?

2 Vocabulary

Find the words in bold in the text and match to these definitions.

1 furniture

1 Things in a house like beds, chairs and tables.
2 Cars and other vehicles in one place.
3 A very large farm in Australia or America.
4 A small house in the country.
5 A vehicle that people can live in.
6 A tower next to the sea. It usually has a big light.

Grammar spot
Determiners

too many/much + noun
too many stairs (countable)
too much traffic (uncountable)

adjective + enough
not exciting enough
big enough

enough + noun
enough furniture
not enough people

👓 Grammar page 105

❸ Grammar practice

a Look at these words. Put them under the correct heading.

> tourist   money   visitor   homework
> noise   book   water   chair   tree   time

Countable	Uncountable
tourist	money

b Now use *enough* or *too much/many* to complete these sentences.

1 enough

1 We haven't got _____ money. We can't buy that TV.

2 There isn't _____ space for my computer because there are _____ books on my desk.

3 I've got _____ homework. I can't finish it all tonight.

4 There isn't _____ hot water in this bath. I'm cold!

5 It's very busy in the shopping centre and there are _____ people. Let's go home.

❹ Listening

a (2.31) Listen to David. Are these sentences true (T) or false (F)?

1 F

1 David's house has got a huge garden.

2 David's mum thinks that David has got too many books and games in his room.

3 David likes his house because he can ride his bike outside.

4 David sometimes can't sleep at night because it's not quiet enough.

5 David's friends don't live close enough.

b (2.31) Listen again and check your answers.

My English file

Write about where you live. What is it like? Use *too much, too many,* and *(not) enough*.

My Home

I live in a large flat. It's very noisy here. There are too many cars on the street and there is too much noise but it's close enough to the park.

❺ Speaking

What's your school like? Think of three good things and three bad things about your school. Tell your classmate.

Bad things

There's too much traffic outside.

There aren't enough windows.

Good things

It's warm enough in the winter.

The playground is big enough.

❻ Pronunciation

a Put these words under the correct heading /uː/ or /ʌ/.

> view   enough   mum   school   another   too

/uː/	/ʌ/
view	enough

b (2.32) Listen and check your answers.

❼ Check your English

Choose the correct words to complete the sentences.

1 There are too *much/many* people in our house and it hasn't got *enough space/space enough*! It's *too small/small enough*.

2 Our bedroom has got too *much/many* furniture.

3 This house *isn't/is* quiet enough. There's *too much/enough* traffic outside.

4 There *are/aren't* enough flowers in my garden. I want to get some more.

23 The eco-village

Lesson objectives
- Using large numbers
- Talking about processes

① Guessing

a How much rubbish do people in the UK throw away?

1 76,000 tonnes per day.
2 76,000 tonnes per month.
3 76,000 tonnes per year.

b (2.33) Listen and check. Are you surprised?

② Presentation

a (2.34) Listen and read. Complete the text with the words and numbers in the box.

kitchens 17 paper 17.5 food
15 farm 28 electricity Scotland

1 28

Facts and figures

A tonne = 1,000 kilos
% = per cent
17.5 = seventeen point five
(or seventeen and a half)
A million = 1,000,000
A billion = 1,000,000,000

Darcy, 11

Kyle, 13

Did you know ...?

□ ¹_____ million tonnes of rubbish are thrown away every year in the UK. That's the same as 6 million elephants!

□ Only ²_____ % of rubbish in Britain is recycled.

□ ³_____ million plastic bottles are used every day.

□ ⁴_____ billion plastic bags are produced every year.

But in some places, people live in eco-villages, where lots of things are reused and recycled. Darcy and Kyle live in an eco-village called Melford, in ⁵_____.

Fruit and vegetables are grown at the village ⁸_____ for everyone in the village. 70% of Melford's ⁹_____ is produced here.

The houses are specially designed. They don't use much gas and electricity. They are kept warm with special ⁶_____ in the walls. ⁷_____ and laundry rooms are shared so that very little energy is used.

100% of their ¹⁰_____ is made in Melford. They make their own power with wind turbines.

b (2.34) Listen again and check.

❸ Comprehension

Read about Melford again. Are these sentences true or false? Correct the false sentences.

1 T

1 The UK doesn't recycle a lot of its rubbish.
2 Melford is the name of a house in Scotland.
3 The houses at Melford use a lot of gas and electricity.
4 There is special paper in the walls of the houses.
5 70% of the village's food is not produced at Melford.
6 Melford's power comes from wind turbines.

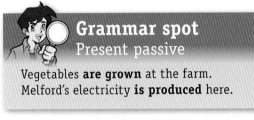

Grammar spot
Present passive

Vegetables **are grown** at the farm.
Melford's electricity **is produced** here.

🔗 Grammar page 105

❹ Class poll

What do you think about Melford? Would you like to live there? Have a class vote. Write the results on the board.

Yes	No

❺ Grammar practice

a Complete these passive sentences with the correct form of the verb in brackets.

1 A lot of things are recycled at Melford.

1 A lot of things (recycle) _____ at Melford.
2 Electricity (produce) _____ for the village.
3 The houses (build) _____ from wood.
4 Vegetables (grow) _____ at the farm.
5 The kitchens (share) _____.

b (2.35) Listen and check.

❻ Listening

a (2.36) Darcy is talking about how her fleece top is made. Listen and put the pictures in the correct order.

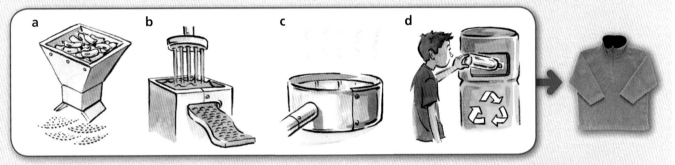

b (2.36) Listen again and complete the sentences. Use the passive form of the verbs in the box.

make   melt   collect   dry   pull   cut   clean

1 are collected

1 First, old plastic bottles _____ from recycling bins.
2 Then they _____ up into very small pieces.
3 The pieces _____ and then they _____.
4 After that, they _____.
5 The melted plastic _____ into long, thin strings.
6 The fleece material _____ from these strings.

❼ Check your English

Match the phrases in A with the phrases in B to make sentences.

A
1 Fruit and vegetables
2 12.5 million tonnes of paper and cardboard
3 This fleece top
4 Old plastic bottles
5 The houses in Melford

B
a is made from recycled plastic bottles.
b are built from wood.
c are collected from recycling bins.
d are grown on a farm near the village.
e are used in the UK every year.

24 The eco-family

❶ Reading

a 2.37 Listen and read the article. Match the questions to the correct answers.

1 *What's your family like?*

What's your home like?   What's your school like?   What's your family like?   What do you usually eat?

In this week's issue of 'My Life', we talk to
Chloe Evans

1 ____
We're a big family. I've got four brothers and three sisters! My mum is an artist and my dad works at home. He's a researcher. My gran also lives with us. Sometimes I think there are too many people in our family – there are eleven people in our house!

2 ____
We live in the Rhondda Valley in Wales. Our house is big enough for our family and we've got a fantastic garden. In our garden we've got a goat and a few chickens! The goat's called Milly. She eats everything in our garden: the flowers, the grass, sometimes even our clothes!

3 ____
We grow our own food. We have fruit trees and a special vegetable garden. We have eggs from our chickens and milk from our goat. We make our own cheese. It's made from Milly's milk!

4 ____
We don't go to school.
Our mum and dad teach us at home. Art is taught by Mum, of course, and all the other subjects are taught by Dad. We do lots of interesting things every day but we always do Maths and English.

b Read the article again and find the answers to these questions.

1 How many people are there in Chloe's family?
2 Where does Chloe live?
3 Who is Milly?
4 Where does Chloe go to school?
5 Who teaches Art?

❷ Listening

a (2.38) Listen to this interview with Fred Braithwaite. Find and correct the seven mistakes below.

my two sisters

Hello, Fred. Tell us about yourself.

Hi. Well, there are four people in my family. There's me, my two brothers and my mum.

And what's your home like?

We live in a big flat in Glasgow, Scotland. There's too much space for four people really, but it's a nice place. We don't have a garden but we have a great view of the city. Oh, and we've got two crazy dogs called Ginger and Tilly.

What do you usually eat, Fred?

We eat very healthy food. We don't eat too many chips or chocolate. We have lots of fruit and vegetables, pasta and cheese.

What's your school like?

It's OK, but there are too many desks in my class! There are thirty-two students and there's only one teacher!

b (2.38) Listen again and check your answers.

❸ Speaking

Work in pairs.

Student A: You are a reporter for 'My Life' magazine. Interview Student B about his/her life. Ask questions about family/home/school.

Student B: You are an unusual person. Answer Student A's questions about your life. Make up some interesting facts! You can use the ideas below:

> I'm … an alien/a Hollywood star/a famous footballer/an explorer
>
> I live in … a space rocket/a castle/ a house with a gym/a tent
>
> I've got … not much space/a lot of money/ a few pets/not much furniture

Study tip
Remembering vocabulary

Write down words in lexical groups.

Animals	Garden
chicken	flowers
goat	grass

❹ Writing

Write about your unusual life. Use the facts you made up for Activity 3. Start like this:

I'm a/an … I live in …

Word race

Play in teams. How many more words can you write for each heading?
You have three minutes.
The team with the most words is the winner!

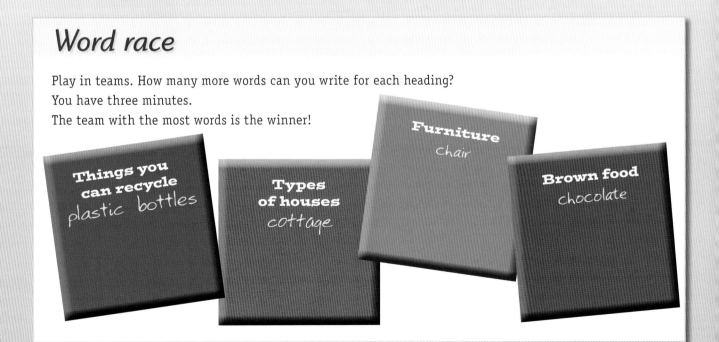

Things you can recycle
plastic bottles

Types of houses
cottage

Furniture
chair

Brown food
chocolate

Review

Check you can do these things.

1 I know words about DIY.
Write the things. Use the initial letters to help you.

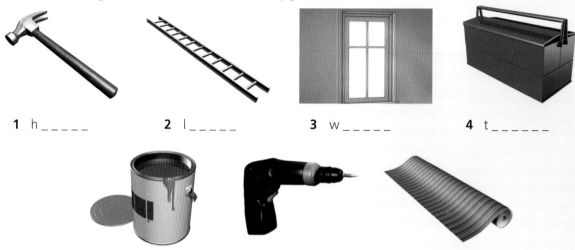

1 h _ _ _ _ _

2 l _ _ _ _ _

3 w _ _ _ _ _

4 t _ _ _ _ _ _

5 p _ _ _ _

6 d _ _ _ _

7 w _ _ _ _ _ _ _ _

2 I can make predictions about the future.
Use *going to* and a verb from the box to complete these sentences.

    break   spill   drop   eat   fall off   trip over

1 She _____ the ice cream.

3 He _____ the water.

5 He _____ the plate.

2 They _____ the dog.

4 She _____ the books.

6 The cat _____ the tree.

❸ I know words for different types of homes.

Complete the word grid. What is the mystery word?

1 a big farm in America or Australia
2 a place where people live
3 a tall building near the sea with a bright light
4 a home with wheels

				³l			
¹r							
		²h		⁴c			
			t		g	e	

❹ I know the difference between countable and uncountable nouns.

Write *too many* before each countable noun and *too much* before each uncountable noun.

1 _____ traffic
2 _____ people
3 _____ cars
4 _____ noise
5 _____ furniture
6 _____ money
7 _____ games
8 _____ visitors

❺ I can talk about quantity.

Choose the correct word to complete this text.

There are too ¹ *many/much* tourists in my village and it's ² *too/enough* noisy. I want to move but we don't have ³ *many/enough* money. Our house isn't big ⁴ *much/enough* and there isn't ⁵ *many/enough* space in the garden, either. My mum says I've got too ⁶ *much/many* games in my room and it's not ⁷ *many tidy/tidy enough*.

❻ I can talk about processes.

Use the passive form of the verb in brackets to complete these sentences about Melford.

1 Electricity _____ (produce) by wind turbines.
2 Vegetables _____ (grow) in the fields.
3 The houses _____ (keep) warm with special paper in the walls.
4 Kitchens and laundry rooms _____ (share).
5 A lot of things _____ (reuse) and _____ (recycle).

> **Extra reading**
> Turn to page 96 and read
> an extract from *Jane Eyre*.

Extra special

Mini-play

Look at the picture. What is Jane doing?

a (2.39) Listen and read. Who has an accident?

Jane   Mark, I need a few things. Can you go to the shops for me?

Mark   What do you need?

Jane   I need a little more paint. And I need another paintbrush.

Mark   Why? What are you doing?

Jane   I'm painting the window.

Mark   Why are you painting the window?

Jane   Because it's old and dirty.

Mark   Well, I don't think it's a good idea.

Jane   Why not?

Mark	Well … it's dangerous.
Jane	No, it's not!
Mark	Watch out! You're going to fall off the ladder!
Jane	No, I'm not! I'm fine.
Mark	Well, be careful. You're going to spill the paint!
Jane	Don't be silly. I'm not going to fall off the ladder and I'm not going to spill the paint.
Mark	OK, OK. I'm sorry. But you usually have a lot of accidents.
Jane	Accidents? No, I don't. I never have accidents.
Mark	Yes, you do. You … STOP!
Jane	What?
Mark	You're going to break the window with your paintbrush!
Jane	No, I'm not! Really, Mark, calm down. Look, I haven't got enough paint here. Can you get some more?
Mark	Oh well, OK.
Jane	Thank you!
Mark	Watch out! You're going to drop your paintbrush onto the floor.
Jane	Mark! Stop it! I'm not going to fall off the ladder. I'm not going to spill the paint. I'm not going to break the window and I'm not going to drop my paintbrush on the floor.
Mark	Hmm. OK. Look, here's the paint and the new paintbrush. I'll bring it over to you.
Jane	No, Mark, wait! I think that's a bad idea.
Mark	Why?
Jane	Because you're going to …
Mark	Ow!
Jane	… trip over the paint pot!

b (2.39) Listen again. Then choose your part: Jane or Mark and read the play with a classmate.

Memory challenge
Learn your lines by heart.

Mini-project

1 Read Shivani's general knowledge quiz. Write answers to the questions.

General knowledge quiz

Honda cars are made in …
A Sweden   **B** Japan   **C** France

Paper is made from …
A grass   **B** hair   **C** wood

Cocoa beans are grown in …
A Austria   **B** Kenya   **C** Canada

Omelettes are made with …
A rice   **B** eggs   **C** sugar

Glass is made from …
A sand   **B** plastic   **C** water

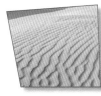 

Shivani

2 Write a general knowledge quiz. Use the present passive.

3 Ask your classmates to write answers to your quiz.

25 Rules of the road

❶ Presentation

a (2.40) Listen and read. Match the traffic rules with the Glooms. Write the letters.

1 f

Traffic rules

1 You mustn't drive more than 30 mph.
2 You must stop when the traffic light is red.
3 You mustn't enter this street.
4 You must keep straight on. You mustn't turn left.
5 You mustn't park here.
6 You must cycle in the cycle lane. You mustn't cycle on the pavement.
7 You must wear a crash helmet when you ride a motorbike.
8 You mustn't cross the road. You must wait for the green man.

b (2.40) Listen again and check your answers. Then point to the Glooms in the picture and read out the traffic rules.

You mustn't cross the road. You must wait for the green man.

Grammar spot
Obligation *must, mustn't*

You **must stop** when the traffic light is red.
You **mustn't turn** left.

(78)

📖 Grammar page 105

❷ Grammar practice

Look at the traffic signs. Make sentences with *You must/mustn't* and these words.

> turn left   stop   wear a crash helmet
> cross the road   park   keep straight on

> *You must keep straight on.*

1   2   3   4   5   6

❸ Vocabulary

a   **2.41** Look at the picture in Activity 1. Listen and find these things.

parking meter – 4

> parking meter   traffic sign
> cycle lane   pedestrian crossing
> traffic lights   traffic warden
> pavement   crossroads

b   **2.42** Listen and check.

❹ Speaking

a   Look at the map. Find *You are here* and follow the instructions. What are the missing words?

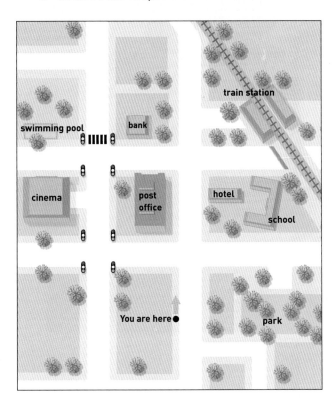

> *Excuse me, where is the _____, please?*

> *Turn left at the crossroads. Keep straight on until the traffic lights and turn right. Then keep straight on until the pedestrian crossing. Cross the road. Keep straight on. The _____ is on the right.*

b   **2.43** Listen and check.

c   Work with a classmate. Take it in turns to give directions to the different places on the map. Use the phrases in the box to help you.

> turn left/right   keep straight on (until)
> cross the road   it's on the left/right
> walk along (the road)

> *Excuse me, where is the bank, please?*

> *Walk along the road and turn right at the ...*

❺ Class poll

a   In groups think about where you live and write some traffic rules on the board. Use *You must ...* or *You mustn't ...*

> You must stop when the
> traffic light is red.
>
> You mustn't drive on the left.

b   Look at your ideas and vote for the rule you think is the most important.

❻ Check your English

a   Complete the sentences with *must* or *mustn't* and an appropriate verb.

In my country …

1   You _____ a crash helmet when you ride a motorbike.
2   You _____ in the cycle lane.
3   You _____ at more than 50 kph in a city.
4   You _____ when the traffic light is red.

b   Look at the map in Activity 4 and write the instructions from *You are here* to the train station.

Walk along the road ...

26 My secret identity

❶ Presentation.

a (2.44) Listen and read. Is the man's name really Mr King?

Passport Control

1　Name: Anthony Graham King
2　Name of hotel in Sylvania: Ritz Palace Hotel
3　Profession: Artist　How long: for 2 years
4　Pilot's licence　How long: since 2007
5　Address: New York　How long: for 3 months
6　Telephone number: 01 934 857 1006
7　Passport　How long: since August

Guard	Hello, Mr King. Why do you want to visit our country?
Mr King	I'm here to paint pictures of your beautiful mountains.
Guard	But there aren't any mountains in Sylvania, Mr King.
Mr King	Er ... I mean your beautiful countryside.
Guard	Umm ... I think I must ask you some questions. What is your full name?
Mr King	It's Graham Anthony King.
Guard	I see. And where are you staying in Sylvania?
Mr King	At the Ritz Palace Hotel.
Guard	Ah, the Ritz. It's a very good hotel. So, you're an artist, Mr King. How long have you been an artist?
Mr King	I've been an artist for two years.
Guard	Two years? Umm ... and I see you can fly a plane, Mr King.

Mr King	Yes, I can.
Guard	How long have you had a pilot's licence?
Mr King	I've had a pilot's licence since 2008.
Guard	Umm ... since 2008. And how long have you lived in New York?
Mr King	I've lived there for six months.
Guard	For six months? I see. What is your telephone number there?
Mr King	It's ... let's see, er ... 01 834 875 1006.
Guard	Umm. And how long have you had a passport?
Mr King	I've had a passport since August.
Guard	I'm afraid you cannot enter Sylvania. You have made four mistakes and I don't believe you are Mr King ... I think you are the world famous secret agent Mr X.

b (2.44) Look at the information on the computer and listen again. What four mistakes does Mr X make?

Grammar spot
Present perfect with *for* and *since*

How long **have** you **been** an artist?
I**'ve been** an artist **for** two years.
I**'ve lived** there **for** six months.

How long **have** you **had** a pilot's licence?
I**'ve had** a pilot's licence **since** 2008.
I**'ve had** a passport **since** August.

> 👓 **Grammar page 101**

❷ Grammar practice

a Work with a classmate. Copy and complete the lists with the words below.

> six days   Tuesday   a week   ten years
> my birthday   last year   a few minutes
> an hour   1999   February

For	Since
six days	*Tuesday*

b 🔊 **2.45** Listen and check.

❸ Speaking

a Make notes about yourself.

1 I've lived in my home for 13 years.

1 I've lived in my home for …
2 I've been at this school since …
3 I've known my friend ____ for …
4 I've had my Hot Spot book since …

b Work with a classmate. Take it in turns to ask and answer these questions.

> How long have you lived in your home?
> > For thirteen years.

1 How long have you lived in your home?
2 How long have you been at this school?
3 How long have you known your friend ____?
4 How long have you had your Hot Spot book?

c Report back to the class.

> Tomas has lived in his home for thirteen years.

❹ Game

a Work in a small team. Write a secret agent's identity. Fill in the form below.

1	Name:	
2	Name of hotel in Sylvania:	
3	Profession:	How long: **for** …
4	Driving licence:	How long: **for** …
5	Address:	How long: **since** …
6	Telephone number:	
7	Passport:	How long: **since** …
8	Favourite food:	

b Exchange identities with another team. Memorise your new identity. Then give back your identity to the other team.

c Now take it in turns to ask and answer questions. You get 1 point for every correct answer.

> What's your full name?
> > Maria Luisa Gonzales.
> Correct.

❺ Writing

Write a dialogue between a border guard and a secret agent. Use your secret identity from Activity 4 to help you.

> A: What is your full name?
> B: My full name is Maria Luisa Gonzales.
> A: Where are you staying in Sylvania?
> B: I'm staying at the …

❻ Check your English

a Work with a classmate. Use your information from Activity 4. Ask and answer.

> What is her name?
> > Maria Luisa Gonzales.
> Where is she staying?
> > At the Queen Hotel.

b Complete these sentences with *for* or *since*.

1 I've had my bag ____ two years.
2 My sister has worked in a shop ____ April.
3 My brother has played football ____ he was six.
4 We have studied English ____ three years.

27 My amazing year

Lesson objectives
- Describing recent experiences
- Talking about plans for the future

❶ Vocabulary

2.46 Find these things in the pictures.

Malaysian food   belt   tomato   balcony   seeds   pot

❷ Presentation

a **2.47** Listen and read Charlie's web page. Which experience or plan do you think is the most interesting?

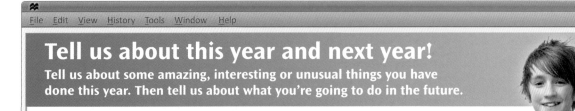

File   Edit   View   History   Tools   Window   Help

Tell us about this year and next year!
Tell us about some amazing, interesting or unusual things you have done this year. Then tell us about what you're going to do in the future.

My name's Charlie Fisher and I'm thirteen years old.

What have I done this year?

■ I've joined a karate club and I've got my orange belt! I started lessons in February – it's hard work but it's also great fun.

■ I've eaten Malaysian food. I went to my friend Mel's house last weekend. Mel's mum is from Malaysia and she cooked a typical Malaysian meal with rice, chicken and peanuts. It was delicious!

■ I've started guitar lessons. My dad gave me his old guitar. I can play six chords now and I've written a song. Hey – I'm going to be a pop star!

What am I going to do next year?

■ I'm going to form a band with some of my friends. Mel's a really good singer and Mike can play drums. We're going to be famous!

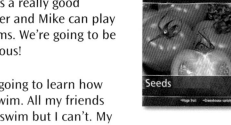

Seeds

■ I'm going to learn how to swim. All my friends can swim but I can't. My Uncle Pete's going to teach me how to swim during the summer holidays. I'm a bit scared!

■ I'm going to grow some vegetables! We don't have a garden, but I can grow tomatoes in small pots on our balcony. I'm going to plant the seeds next week. Yum! I love tomatoes!

b Listen again. Then match the words in A to the words in B to make phrases from the text.

	A		B
1	join	**a**	Malaysian food
2	eat	**b**	how to swim
3	learn	**c**	some vegetables
4	grow	**d**	a karate club
5	plant	**e**	the seeds

③ Comprehension

Are these sentences true (T) or false (F)? Correct the false sentences.

1   F Charlie started guitar lessons this year.

1   Charlie's going to learn how to play the guitar next year.
2   He's eaten Malaysian food.
3   He's formed a band with his friends.
4   He's going to plant some tomato seeds next week.
5   He's got his orange belt in karate.

Grammar spot
Present perfect/past simple/ *going to*

Present perfect
I'**ve joined** a karate club.

Past simple
I **started** lessons in February.

going to **for future plans**
I'**m going to form** a band.

> Grammar pages 99, 101, 104

④ Grammar practice

Read and complete Mel's web page. Put the verbs in brackets into the correct tense: present perfect, past simple or *going to*.

1   I've visited
2   I went

What have I done this year?

- I ¹_____ (visit) my friend, Michelle, in France. I ²_____ (go) to her house in Montpellier for Easter.

- I ³_____ (join) the eco-club at school. Last week we ⁴_____ (make) a poster about recycling.

- I ⁵_____ (start) horse riding lessons. I ⁶_____ (have) five lessons in January. They were great!

What am I going to do next year?

- I ⁷_____ (stay) with my aunt in Scotland for the summer holidays. She's got a beautiful little cottage in the Highlands.

- I ⁸_____ (invite) Michelle to stay with me next month. She's never been to the UK.

- I ⁹_____ (learn) how to cook Malaysian food. My mum ¹⁰_____ (teach) me.

⑤ Pronunciation

a (2.48) Listen to this tongue twister.
/g/
Gregory's going to grow gorgeous green grapes in his grandfather's garden.

b (2.49) Listen again and repeat. How fast can you say it?

⑥ Speaking

a   Use the words below to make questions.
1   Have you visited an interesting place this year?

> **What have you done this year?**
> 1   visit/an interesting place
> 2   start/violin/riding/piano/karate lessons
> 3   join/a club
> 4   eat/some unusual food
> 5   get/a new pet

b   Now ask and answer with a classmate.

Have you visited an interesting place this year?

Yes, I have. I've been to Prague. I went …

My English file

a Write about your year. Describe three unusual, interesting or amazing experiences.
I've learnt how to ski. I went to Kamchatka in Russia with my cousins. I've started …

b Write about three plans for next year.
I'm going to join a football team in my village. I'm going to …

⑦ Song

(2.50) Find the song *We are the Champions* on page 91.

⑧ Check your English

Complete these sentences with the present perfect, the past simple or the *going to* form of the verbs in brackets.

1   Next summer I _____ (start) violin lessons.
2   I _____ (form) a band with my brother. We _____ (play) at our first concert last week.
3   I _____ (get) a new cat tomorrow.
4   We _____ (play) basketball next weekend.

28 Amazing places

❶ Reading

a `2.51` Listen and read the emails. What are they about?

> wonderful homes
> interesting buildings in Britain
> unusual holiday places
> amazing fruits

b

Hi John,

Brrr! It's cold! I'm in Oymyakon, Russia – the coldest town in the world! It's -50°C today. I've been here since yesterday and it's fantastic! I'm staying with a family in a log cabin. There's a big festival on at the moment. It's called 'The Pole of Cold Festival'. There are fishing competitions, fireworks and music. Tomorrow, I'm going to watch a reindeer race!

Ben

a

Diana,

Hello from the Pineapple House in Scotland! I've been here for a week and this place is amazing! It's 250 years old and it's got a 23-metre stone pineapple on the roof! You can rent the house for the weekend or for a week. We're having a great time. We've walked around the beautiful gardens, we've visited a castle and tomorrow we're going to take a boat trip.

Carly

c

Susie,

This is an amazing place! It's a hotel in a cave in Cappadocia, Turkey. We've been here for a week and we've seen some fantastic houses in the caves. My bedroom is more than 1400 years old. It's very beautiful, with stone walls and a big window. We're going to go home tomorrow but I want to come back here next year.

Ursula

b Read again. Find words to match these definitions.

1 *Pineapple*

1 (email a) a kind of fruit
2 (email a) pay money to stay in a place
3 (email b) a house made of wood
4 (email c) a large hole in the side of a hill

② Speaking

a Work in small groups. Choose one place from Activity 1 to go on holiday. Why?

> I want to go to … because … is more exciting/unusual/interesting than …

> I don't like cold weather/hot weather/caves so I'd like to …

b Tell the class about your choice.

> We want to go to …

③ Listening

2.52 Teri is talking about her holiday plans. Listen then choose the correct words.

1 Teri is going to stay *in a caravan/in a teepee.*
2 A teepee is a kind of *tent/boat.*
3 Teri and her family are going to *go cycling/go horse riding.*
4 In the evenings they're going to cook their food *on a fire/in a stove.*

④ Writing

a Invent an unusual holiday place. Make notes about these things.

Is it a house/a hotel/a tent?   *How old is it?*
What can you do during the day?   *Is it expensive or cheap?*

b Now imagine you are staying in your holiday place. Write an email to a friend.

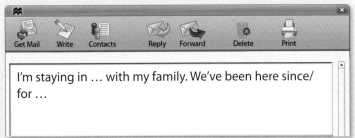

I'm staying in … with my family. We've been here since/ for …

Writing tip

Use adjectives to describe things.

*We've walked around the **beautiful** gardens.*

*I've had some **delicious** hot chocolate.*

Talk about it!

Work in small groups. Throw the dice and land on a segment. Talk about that subject for 30 seconds.

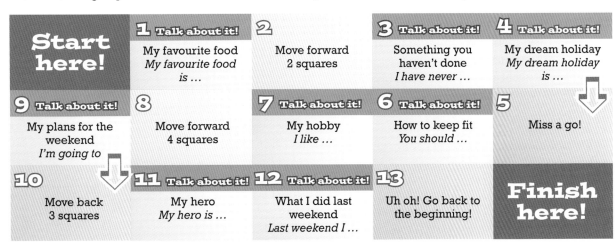

Review

Check you can do these things.

❶ I can use *must* and *mustn't* to talk about traffic rules.

Choose the correct word *must* or *mustn't* to complete these rules.

1

You *must/mustn't* wear a helmet on a moped.

2

You *must/mustn't* cycle on the pavement.

3

You *must/mustn't* cross when you see the red man at a pedestrian crossing.

4

You *must/mustn't* cycle in a cycle lane.

5

You *must/mustn't* wait for the green man at a pedestrian crossing.

6

You *must/mustn't* enter a street with this sign.

❷ I know words for different types of road features.

Find the names of five different types of road features in this word snake.

parkingmetertrafficlightspavementpedestriancrossingtrafficwarden

❸ I can give directions.

Look at the map and complete the directions to the supermarket.

Turn ¹*right/left* out of the hotel and turn ²*right/left* at the traffic lights. Then keep straight ³*on/over* until you get to the ⁴*crossroads/pedestrian crossing*. Turn right and then walk ⁵*along/on* the road until you get to the pedestrian crossing. ⁶*Cross/Walk* the road and the supermarket is next to the school.

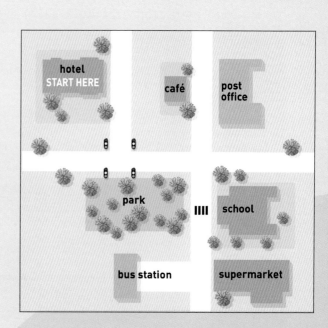

4 I can use *for* and *since* to talk about time.

Complete these time expressions with *for* or *since*.

1 _____ yesterday   **4** _____ 1999
2 _____ four weeks   **5** _____ last April
3 _____ a year   **6** _____ two hours

5 I can use the present perfect to talk about time.

a Write these questions using the present perfect.

1 How long/you/live/in your town?
2 How long/you/be/in this classroom?
3 How long/your teacher/teach at this school?
4 How long/you/have/your schoolbag?

b Now write true answers to the questions above.

I've lived here for four years.

6 I can use the present perfect and the past simple to talk about my experiences.

Write the correct form of the verb in brackets to complete these sentences. Use the present perfect or past simple.

1 I _____ (fly) to Paris. I _____ (visit) my aunt there last Christmas.
2 I _____ (eat) Chinese food. I _____ (go) to a Chinese restaurant in April.
3 I _____ (learn) how to ski. My brother _____ (teach) me last December.
4 I _____ (grow) some tomatoes. I _____ (plant) the seeds two months ago.

7 I can use *going to* to talk about plans for the future.

What are you going to do next year? Tick (✓) at least three things in the list. Then write sentences.

Next year I'm going to ...

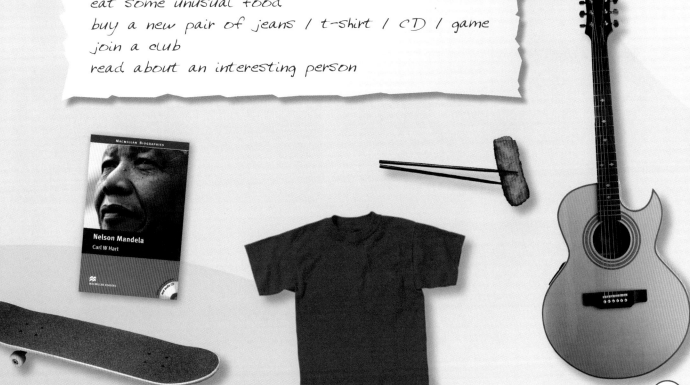

learn a new sport / instrument / skill
visit an aunt / uncle / cousin
eat some unusual food
buy a new pair of jeans / t-shirt / CD / game
join a club
read about an interesting person

Extra special

Hot Spot end of book quiz!

1 Play this game in teams.
2 Write your answers to the questions.
3 Don't worry if you can't remember. You can look in your book!
4 The first team with 15 correct answers is the winner!

1 Why does this boy clap his hands when he leaves the house?

6 What colour is Phoebe's school uniform?

2 Where does this girl live?

7 Why is Sumeo's house on stilts?

3 Who made a hole in Martha Gloom's garden?

8 Can you remember? What does Sophie's dad want to see?

4 Aimee Mullins is a famous athlete. Can you remember her other two jobs?

9 What school did Katie Melua go to?

5 Has Eva ever eaten smelly cheese?

10 Should you open presents immediately in Sun's country?

11 Can you remember? What should you do if you see a bear in front of you?

12 What are the names of these different types of homes?

a b

c d

13 Where does Chloe go to school?

14 Can you write the words for these things?

a b c d

e f

15 How old is this house?

Mini-project

1 Look at Suzie's timeline. How old is she now?

The important times in my life

14 years ago
I was born in Guildford, England.

10 years ago
I started school. I liked school, but I didn't like the uniform!

9 years ago
I learnt how to ride a bike. My first bike was purple. I thought it was cool!

7 years ago
I went on a plane for the first time. I went with my family to Spain on holiday. The holiday was great!

5 years ago
I won a poetry competition. The prize was a big dictionary.

3 years ago
I went on the London to Brighton bike ride with my Mum and Dad. I cycled 70 kilometres in one day!

1 year ago
I went to my first pop concert. I saw Leona Lewis at the O2 Arena in London. It was a fantastic concert!

Suzie

2 Write about the important times in your life.

3 Show your timeline to your classmates.

Songs

I Have a Dream

written by Benny Anderson and Björn Ulvaeus

Have You Ever Seen the Rain?

written by John Fogerty

Someone told me long ago
There's a calm before the storm
I know – and it's been coming for some time
When it's over so they say
It'll rain a sunny day
I know – shining down like water

I want to know
Have you ever seen the rain
I want to know
Have you ever seen the rain
Coming down on a sunny day

Yesterday and days before
Sun is cold and rain is hot
I know – been that way for all my time
'Till forever, on it goes
Through the circle fast and slow
I know – and it can't stop I wonder

I want to know
Have you ever seen the rain
I want to know
Have you ever seen the rain
Coming down on a sunny day

I want to know
Have you ever seen the rain
I want to know
Have you ever seen the rain
Coming down on a sunny day

John Fogerty wrote *Have You Ever Seen the Rain* for the 1970 album, *Pendulum*. This was while he was a member of the band, Creedence Clearwater Revival. Creedence Clearwater Revival was the most successful band in 1970. *Have You Ever Seen the Rain* has also been sung by R.E.M and The Fray.

I have a dream, a song to sing
To help me cope with anything
If you see the wonder of a fairy tale
You can take the future even if you fail
I believe in angels
Something good in everything I see
I believe in angels
When I know the time is right for me
I'll cross the stream – I have a dream

I have a dream, a fantasy
To help me through reality
And my destination makes it worth the while
Pushing through the darkness still another mile
I believe in angels
Something good in everything I see
I believe in angels
When I know the time is right for me
I'll cross the stream – I have a dream
I'll cross the stream – I have a dream

I have a dream, a song to sing
To help me cope with anything
If you see the wonder of a fairy tale
You can take the future even if you fail
I believe in angels
Something good in everything I see
I believe in angels
When I know the time is right for me
I'll cross the stream – I have a dream
I'll cross the stream – I have a dream

Benny Andersson and Björn Ulvaeus were members of the group ABBA. *I Have a Dream* was written by them for the 1979 ABBA album, *Voulez-Vous*. Recently, Amanda Seyfried sang *I Have a Dream* as part of the popular movie *Mamma Mia*.

We are the Champions
written by Freddie Mercury

I've paid my dues –
Time after time –
I've done my sentence
But committed no crime –
And bad mistakes
I've made a few
I've had my share of sand kicked in my face –
But I've come through

We are the champions – my friends
And we'll keep on fighting – till the end –
We are the champions –
We are the champions
No time for losers
'cause we are the champions – of the world –

I've taken my bows
And my curtain calls –
You brought me fame and fortune and everything that goes with it –
I thank you all –

But it's been no bed of roses
No pleasure cruise –
I consider it a challenge before the whole human race –
And I ain't gonna lose –

We are the champions – my friends
And we'll keep on fighting – till the end –
We are the champions –
We are the champions
No time for losers
'cause we are the champions – of the world

Freddie Mercury was the lead singer for the band Queen. He wrote *We are the Champions* for the album, *News of the World*. *We are the Champions* has been a popular song ever since it's release in 1977. In 2009, Queen and their song, *We are the Champions*, were inducted into the Grammy Hall of Fame.

Robinson Crusoe

❶ Before you read

a Read the background information below.

Daniel Defoe wrote 'Robinson Crusoe' in 1719. The story is about a man, Robinson Crusoe. He is on a ship in the sea. There is a bad storm and he swims to an island. There are no other people on the island. He lives there for many years.

b Can you think of any other famous books about ships and the sea?

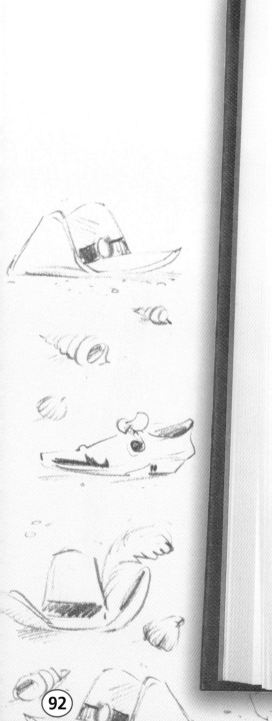

On the night of 20th of November, 1656 there was a terrible storm. Our ship hit some rocks. We got into a small boat, but the waves were too high. We all fell into the sea…

The next morning I woke up on a beach. I looked out to sea and saw our broken ship. Where were my shipmates? I looked around but I couldn't see anyone. The only things I could find on the beach were three hats, a cap and two odd shoes.

My clothes were wet and I had no dry clothes. I was hungry and thirsty and I had nothing to eat or drink. The only things in my pockets were a knife, a pipe and some tobacco in a box.

The sun was very hot. I made an umbrella out of some big leaves from a tree and I walked along the beach. After two hours I found a creek. I filled my hands with fresh water and drank. The water was delicious.

I looked at the sun. I guessed it was about six o'clock in the afternoon. The forest next to the beach was already very dark. Perhaps there were dangerous animals in the forest. I didn't want the wild animals to eat me. I decided to sit in a tree all night and climbed the tallest tree I could find. I didn't want to sleep because I was afraid, but I was very tired and slept all night like a bird in a tree.

The next day I wanted to know more about my situation. I could see a hill in the forest. I thought, 'Perhaps I can see where I am from the top of that hill.' It was difficult to walk and climb to the top of the hill through the thick forest. At the top I looked around. I could see the sea all around me. I looked for a town or some sign of human habitation. There was nothing. I was alone on an island in the middle of the ocean.

❷ Comprehension

Read the text carefully and answer the questions.

  a What did Crusoe find on the beach?
  b What did Crusoe have in his pockets?
  c Where did Crusoe find some water?
  d Why did Crusoe sleep in a tree?

❸ Discussion

Work in groups. Imagine you are on an island. You will be alone on this island for two years. Discuss these questions.

  1 You can take three books onto your island. Which books do you choose? Why?
  2 You can watch three films on your island. Which films do you choose? Why?
  3 You can eat three different types of food on your island. Which types of food do you choose? Why?

The Adventures of Tom Sawyer

❶ Before you read

a Read the background information below.

Mark Twain (real name: Samuel Langhorne Clemens) is the author of 'The Adventures of Tom Sawyer'. He wrote the book in 1876. The hero, Tom Sawyer, is a young boy who lives in Missouri, USA. He is very naughty and always gets into trouble!

b Can you think of any other famous books with children as the main characters?

It was Saturday morning. There was no school today. But Tom had to work. He had to paint the fence. It was a long fence around the garden of Aunt Polly's house.

Tom had a big bucket of paint and a brush with a long handle. He looked at the fence.

'I want to go swimming. I want to go fishing. I want to play with my friends,' Tom said to himself. 'I don't want to paint the fence. My friends will all see me. They'll laugh at me.'

Tom started to paint.

After an hour, Tom was tired. He looked sadly at the big bucket of paint and the brush with the long handle. Then Tom had an idea. He smiled.

He started to paint the fence again.

Soon he saw one his friends, Ben Rogers.

Ben was holding a big red apple.

'I'm going swimming,' Ben said. 'You have to work!'

'I'm not working,' said Tom. 'This isn't work!'

'Do you like painting the fence?' asked Ben. He was surprised.

'Yes,' said Tom.

Tom started to paint again. Sometimes he stopped and looked at the fence. Then he painted again. There was a happy smile on his face.

Ben watched him. 'Let me paint the fence,' he said.

'No,' said Tom. 'It's very difficult to paint a fence.'

Ben was not happy. Tom liked painting the fence. So Ben wanted to paint the fence.

'Please let me paint it,' he said. 'I'll give you some of my apple.'

Tom thought for a moment. 'No,' he replied. And he smiled and started to paint again.

'I'll give you all of my apple,' said Ben.

Tom thought for another minute. 'All right,' he said.

So Tom sat down and started to eat Ben's apple. And Ben started to paint the fence.

After an hour, Ben was tired. He gave the bucket, the paint and the brush to Tom. Then he went away.

② Comprehension

Read the text carefully. Are the sentences true (T) or false (F)?

a Tom wants to paint the fence.
b Ben Rogers wants to paint the fence.
c Ben gives some of his apple to Tom.
d Billy Fisher doesn't want to paint the fence.

③ Discussion.

Work in groups. Discuss these questions.

a Is it fun or boring to paint a fence?
b Tom Sawyer's friends paint the fence for Tom. Is Tom clever or naughty?

Then Tom saw another friend, Billy Fisher. Billy was holding a kite. 'Ben was painting your fence,' said Billy. 'Let me paint your fence.'

'No,' replied Tom. 'Lots of boys want to paint my fence. But it's very difficult to paint a fence.'

'Oh,' said Billy.

'Ben gave me his apple,' said Tom. 'Then he painted the fence.'

'I'll give you my kite,' said Billy.

Tom thought for a minute. 'All right,' he said.

So Tom sat down. He was holding Billy's kite. And Billy started to paint the fence.

The morning passed. The fence was painted twice. Tom had a kite, a cat and a long piece of rope. He had a cake, twelve round stones and a metal door-handle. He was happy. He went to speak to Aunt Polly.

'The fence is painted,' he said. 'And there is no more paint.'

Aunt Polly was very surprised. 'You are a good boy, Tom,' she said.

Jane Eyre

1 Before you read

a Read the background information below.

Charlotte Brontë wrote the novel, 'Jane Eyre' in 1847. It is the story of a girl. Her parents are dead and she lives with her aunt and cousins. When she is ten years old, her aunt sends her to Lowood School.

b Can you name any famous authors from your country who lived at the same time as Charlotte Brontë?

It was the month of January. I arrived at Lowood School at night. A servant took me up some stairs and into a big bedroom. There were many beds in the room. The girls in the beds were asleep. The servant took me to an empty bed. I put on my nightclothes and I got into bed. Soon, I was asleep too.

I woke up very early. A loud bell was ringing. The bedroom was dark and cold. I watched the other girls. They washed in cold water and they dressed quickly.

There was a plain brown dress next to my bed and there was a pair of ugly, heavy shoes. I washed quickly. Then I put on my new clothes.

I was very hungry. I followed the other girls down the stairs. We sat down at long tables in a large dining room. Our food was terrible.

'The food is bad again,' one of the girls said.

'Stand up!' a teacher shouted. 'Don't talk!'

We stood up. We did not speak. We walked into a big schoolroom and we sat down.

There were about eighty girls in the schoolroom. And there were four classes. The oldest girls were in the fourth class. I was in the first class.

Four teachers came into the room and we began our lessons. The lessons were not interesting. First, we read some pages in a book. Then our teacher asked us questions about those pages.

After four hours, we went outside. It was very cold. Very soon, a bell rang. Lessons started again.

…

Three weeks passed. One afternoon, the head teacher came into the schoolroom. The head teacher's name was Miss Temple. Mr Brocklehurst was with her. We all stood up. I stood behind an older girl. I did not want Mr Brocklehurst to see me.

Mr Brocklehurst walked slowly round the room. Everybody was very quiet. And then I dropped my book!

Mr Brocklehurst stopped walking. He looked at me.

'Ah! The new girl,' he said. 'Come here, Jane Eyre.' Then he pointed at two of the older girls. 'You girls – put Jane Eyre on that high chair!' he said.

❷ Comprehension

Read the text carefully then put the events in the correct order.

a ___ The girls began their lessons.
b ___ Jane stood on a high chair.
c ___ Jane arrived at Lowood.
d ___ The head teacher and Mr Brocklehurst came into the schoolroom.
e ___ The girls sat in a large dining room.

❸ Discussion

Work in groups. Discuss these questions:
a The text describes a school in the 1840s. How is it different from a modern school?
b What do you think? What is the worst thing about the school in the text?

'Look at Jane Eyre, everybody!' Mr Brocklehurst said. 'This child is bad. She is a liar. She will be punished! Miss Temple! Teachers! Girls! Do not talk to this child!'

Then he spoke to me again.

'Jane Eyre, you must stand on that chair for two hours,' he said. 'You are a bad girl!'

That evening, I cried and cried. But Miss Temple was kind to me.

'You are a good pupil, Jane,' she said. 'And you are not a bad girl. I am your friend, Jane.'

'Thank you, Miss Temple,' I said.

Grammar summary

❶ Present simple

We use the present simple to talk about facts that are generally true.

> Sun **doesn't live** in England. She **lives** in China.

We also use the present simple to talk about things that happen repeatedly, for example, *every morning*, *usually*, *always* or *sometimes*.

> I **get up** at seven o'clock every morning.

> **Do** you always **walk** to school? — Yes, I do.

Check your grammar

Make questions with these words. Then answer about yourself with full sentences.

1 Do you read a lot of books?
Yes, I read a lot of books.
or
No, I don't read a lot of books.

1 you/read/a lot of books
2 your friends/live/near you
3 it/snow/a lot in your country
4 your teacher/give/you a lot of homework
5 you/like/chocolate

❷ Present continuous

We use the present continuous to talk about future arrangements.

> What **are** you **doing** next weekend?

> I**'m visiting** my grandparents.

> **Is** she **playing** netball on Friday?

We also use the present continuous to talk about things that are happening at the moment we speak.

> What **are** you **eating**?

> I**'m eating** an apple.

> She **isn't doing** her homework.

Check your grammar

What are your plans and arrangements for the future? Make true sentences about you.

1 I'm going out this evening.
or
I'm not going out this evening.

1 go out/this evening
2 visit/relatives/this weekend
3 meet/my friends/tomorrow
4 stay/at home/on Friday night

❸ Possessive pronouns

The possessive pronouns are:

Singular	Plural
mine	ours
yours	yours
his
hers	theirs

Notice how we use possessive pronouns.

> My name's Jake. What's **yours**?

> This isn't Mary's T-shirt. **Hers** is blue.

> Are those your shoes? — No, these are **mine**.

Check your grammar

Make sentences with *This is/These are … mine/ours/yours/his/hers/theirs.*

1 This is yours.

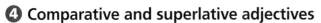

④ Comparative and superlative adjectives

We use comparatives to compare two people or things.

> I'm **older** than my sister.

> Your book is **more interesting** than my book.

We use superlative adjectives to compare three or more people or things.

> I'm the **oldest** student in my class.

> This is the **most interesting** book in the library.

Short adjectives:

Adjective	Comparative	Superlative
tall	tall**er**	tall**est**
old	old**er**	old**est**

Short adjectives ending in a vowel + a consonant:

Adjective	Comparative	Superlative
big	big**ger**	big**gest**
fit	fit**ter**	fit**test**

Short adjectives ending in a y:

Adjective	Comparative	Superlative
funny	funn**ier**	funn**iest**
happy	happ**ier**	happ**iest**

Longer adjectives:

Adjective	Comparative	Superlative
comfortable	**more** comfortable	**most** comfortable
talkative	**more** talkative	**most** talkative

Irregular adjectives:

Adjective	Comparative	Superlative
good	**better**	**best**
bad	**worse**	**worst**

Check your grammar

Make sentences with the comparative or the superlative.

1 I am older than my friend.
2 I am the oldest.

1 I/my friend (old)
2 I/my friend/my classmate (old)
3 a chocolate bar/a sweet (expensive)
4 a chocolate bar/a sweet/chewing gum (expensive)
5 English/Geography (interesting)
6 English/Geography/Science (interesting)

⑤ Past simple

We use the past simple to talk about a definite time in the past.

> Marie and Pierre Curie **discovered** radium.

> **Did** you **win** the race? Yes, I **did**.

We often use past time expressions with the past simple, for example, *yesterday, last weekend, in 2002.*

> We **didn't play** tennis last weekend, we **played** football.

> She **went** to Paris in 2002.

Check your grammar

Make questions with the past simple. Then answer about yourself.

1 Did you meet your friends last weekend?
Yes, I did. or *No. I didn't*

1 meet/your friends/last weekend?
2 watch/TV/last night?
3 swim/in the sea/last year?
4 go to bed early/yesterday?
5 make/your bed/this morning?

Check your grammar

What did you do last weekend? Write sentences about yourself with the past simple.

I met my friends last weekend. We went to the café for lunch. After lunch, ...

❻ Past continuous

We use the past continuous to talk about things that were happening at a particular moment in the past.

> *What **were** you **doing** yesterday at six o'clock?*

> *I **was listening** to music.*

Affirmative sentences:

I **was playing**.
You **were playing**.
He **was playing**.
She **was playing**.
It **was playing**.
We **were playing**.
You **were playing**.
They **were playing**.

Negative sentences:

Full form	Short form
I was **not playing**.	I **wasn't playing**.
You were **not playing**.	You **weren't playing**.
He was **not playing**.	He **wasn't playing**.
She **was playing**.	She **wasn't playing**.
It **was not playing**.	It **wasn't playing**.
We **were not playing**.	We **weren't playing**.
You **were not playing**.	You **weren't playing**.
They **were not playing**.	You **weren't playing**.

Questions and short answers:

Question	Short answers
Was I playing?	Yes, I **was**./No, I **wasn't**.
Were you playing?	Yes, you **were**./No, you **weren't**.
Was he playing? **Was** she playing? **Was** it playing?	Yes, he/she/it **was**. No, he/she/it **wasn't**.
Were we playing? **Were** you playing? **Were** they playing?	Yes, we/you/they **were**. No, we/you/they **weren't**.

Check your grammar

What were Ben and Kate doing yesterday evening at seven thirty? Make sentences using the past continuous.

1 Ben wasn't watching TV.

1 Ben/not/watch/TV
2 They/eat
3 Kate/not/stand up
4 They/not/do/their homework
5 They/not/drink/cola
6 Kate/watch/TV
7 Ben/read/magazine

❼ Past continuous and past simple

We often use the past continuous in the same sentence with the past simple and *when*.

> *I **was sleeping** when the alarm **rang** at seven.*

Check your grammar

Make sentences using the past continuous and past simple.

1 He was skateboarding when he fell over.

1 He/skateboard/when/he/fall/over
2 We/have/a picnic/when/it/start/to rain
3 They/swim/when/they/see/a shark
4 I/look/out of the window/when/it/began/to snow
5 She/tell/a joke/when/the teacher/come/into the room

⑧ Present perfect

We use the present perfect simple to talk about experiences in our lives up to now. We often use *ever* and *never* with this use.

Have you ever **read** Harry Potter?

No, **I've** never **read** it.

We use the present perfect to talk about things that have recently happened. We sometimes use *just* with this use.

My friend **has** just **broken** his leg.

Have you **had** a haircut? Yes, I **have**.

We use the present perfect with *for* and *since* to talk about how long things have continued.

How long **have** you **been** here?

I've been here for *ten minutes*.

My mother **has lived** in this house since *I was six*.

Notice the past participle of regular verbs ends in *-ed*. Some verbs have irregular past participle forms.

👓 **Irregular verbs table page 106**

Affirmative sentences:

Full form			Short form		
I You We You They	have	worked.	I You We You They	've	worked.
He She It	has		He She It	's	

Negative sentences:

Full form			Short form		
I You We You They	have not	worked.	I You We You They	haven't	worked.
He She It	has not		He She It	hasn't	

Questions and short answers:

Question			Short answers
Have	I you we they	worked?	Yes, I/you/we/they **have**. No, I/you/we/they **haven't**.
Has	he she it		Yes, he/she/it **has**. No, he/she/it **hasn't**.

Check your grammar

Make questions with the present perfect. Then answer about youself.

1 Have you ever gone skiing? Yes, I have.

1 ever/go/skiing?
2 ever/ride/a horse?
3 ever/fly/in a plane?
4 ever/meet/a famous person?
5 ever/break you leg?

Check your grammar

Answer these questions with the present perfect and the words in brackets.

1 I've just heard a funny story.

1 What did you just hear? (just/hear/a funny story)
2 What did you just eat? (just/eat/lots of sweets)
3 What did you just lose? (just/lose/my purse)
4 What did you just do? (just/be/on a long walk)

Check your grammar

Choose the correct word *for* or *since*.

1 I've had these jeans for two years.

1 I've had these jeans *for/since* two years.
2 My cousin has been ill *for/since* last Saturday.
3 We've lived in this village *for/since* a long time.
4 I've known my best friend *for/since* I was 12.
5 Megan's played football *for/since* six years.

9 Future predictions with *will*

We use *will* to predict what we think or know will happen in the future.

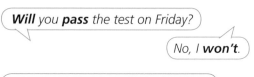

Will you **pass** the test on Friday?

No, I **won't**.

I think we**'ll win** the football match.

Affirmative sentences:

Full form	Short form
I **will** work.	I**'ll** work.
You **will** work.	You**'ll** work.
He **will** work.	He**'ll** work.
She **will** work.	She**'ll** work.
It **will** work.	It**'ll** work.
We **will** work.	We**'ll** work.
You **will** work.	You**'ll** work.
They **will** work.	They**'ll** work.

Negative sentences:

Full form	Short form
I **will not work.**	I **won't work.**
You **will not work.**	You **won't work.**
He **will not work.**	He **won't work.**
She **will not work.**	She **won't work.**
It **will not work.**	It **won't work.**
We **will not work.**	We **won't work.**
You **will not work.**	You **won't work.**
They **will not work.**	They **won't work.**

Questions and short answers:

Question	Short answers
Will I **work**?	
Will you **work**?	
Will he **work**?	
Will she **work**?	Yes, I/you/he/she/it/we/they **will**.
Will it **work**?	No, I/you/he/she/it/we/they **won't**.
Will we **work**?	
Will you **work**?	
Will they **work**?	

Check your grammar

Use *will* and the phrases in brackets to make sentences about the future.

1 It's cold. I think it'll snow tomorrow.

1 It's very cold. (snow tomorrow)
2 I like pop music. (buy a CD)
3 The school's netball team is good. (win the match)
4 My mum's birthday is on Friday. (make a cake)
5 I like Chemistry. (be a scientist)

10 can, could, I'll (requests, offers)

We use *can* and *could* to make requests.

Could you **pass** me the book, please?

Yes, of course.

Can I **switch** on the light?

Sure.

Notice: *could* is more polite than *can*.

We use *I'll* to make offers.

I'll fetch you a glass of water.

Notice: *I'll* = *I will*.

Check your grammar

Match the words in A with the words in B to make an offer or a request.

	A	B
1	I'll	the window.
2	Can you close	get you a drink.
3	Could you pass	the door, please?
4	I'll open	me the pen?

⑪ Making suggestions

We can make suggestions with *How about,*
Let's or *Would you like to.*

> **How about** *meeting in the park?*

> **Let's** *go to the cinema.*

> **Would you like to** *watch TV?*

Notice: *How about* + *-ing,*
Let's and *Would you like to* + infinitive.

Check your grammar

Make suggestions with *How about, Let's* or
Would you like to.

1 How about meeting our friends?

1 _____ meeting our friends?
2 _____ go to the supermarket.
3 _____ see the show?
4 _____ watch TV.
5 _____ playing football?

⑫ First conditional

We use the first conditional to talk about
possible present or future events.

> **If** *my friends* **are** *late, they* **won't see** *the film.*

> **If** *you* **leave** *now, you***'ll catch** *the bus.*

Notice the form for the first conditional.
If + present simple, *will* + infinitive.

Check your grammar

Match the words in A and B and make first
conditional sentences.

1 If it rains, I won't go out.

	A		**B**
1	If it rains,	a	you won't pass the exam.
2	If you go to bed early,	b	I'll go to the beach.
3	If we don't run,	c	I'll do some shopping.
4	If I go out,	d	we won't catch the bus.
5	If you don't study,	e	I won't go out.
6	If it's sunny,	f	you won't be tired tomorrow.

⑬ may (possibility)

We use *may* to say that perhaps something will
happen in the future.

> *I* **may** *go shopping tomorrow*
> *or I* **may not** *go shopping.*

Affirmative sentences	Negative sentences
I **may** go out.	I **may not** go out.
You **may** go out.	You **may not** go out.
He **may** go out.	He **may not** go out.
She **may** go out.	She **may not** go out.
It **may** go out.	It **may not** go out.
We **may** go out.	We **may not** go out.
You **may** go out.	You **may not** go out.
They **may** go out.	They **may not** go out.

Check your grammar

Change these sentences to possibilities using
may.

1 It may rain tomorrow.

1 It's going to rain tomorrow.
2 My friend is going to phone me.
3 I won't go to school today.
4 We will go on holiday this summer.
5 I will buy some new jeans.

⑭ *should, shouldn't* (obligation and advice)

We use *should* and *shouldn't* to give advice and say what we think is good and right.

> *You look ill. You **shouldn't** go to school today. You **should** stay at home.*

> *I **shouldn't** eat so many sweets.*

Affirmative sentences:

I **should** work.
You **should** work.
He **should** work.
She **should** work.
It **should** work.
We **should** work.
You **should** work.
They **should** work.

Negative sentences:

Full form	Short form
I **should not** work.	I **shouldn't** work.
You **should not** work.	You **shouldn't** work.
He **should not** work.	He **shouldn't** work.
She **should not** work.	She **shouldn't** work.
It **should not** work.	It **shouldn't** work.
We **should not** work.	We **shouldn't** work.
You **should not** work.	You **shouldn't** work.
They **should not** work.	They **shouldn't** work.

Questions and short answers:

Question	Short answers
Should I work?	Yes, I **should**. No, I **shouldn't**.
Should you work?	Yes, you **should**. No, you **shouldn't**.
Should he work?	Yes, he **should**. No, he **shouldn't**.
Should she work?	Yes, she **should**. No, she **shouldn't**.
Should it work?	Yes, it **should**. No, it **shouldn't**.
Should we work?	Yes, we **should**. No, we **shouldn't**.
Should you work?	Yes, you **should**. No, you **shouldn't**.
Should they work?	Yes, they **should**. No, they **shouldn't**.

Check your grammar

Make sentences about school with *should* and *shouldn't*.

1 You should do your homework.

1 do your homework
2 eat in the classroom
3 shout
4 listen to your teacher
5 write in your coursebook

⑮ Future predictions with *going to*

We use *going to* to make predictions from what we can see or hear now.

> *The plane **is going to** land.*

We also use *going to* for future plans and intentions.

> *I'**m going to** learn how to play the guitar.*

> *She'**s going to** have a party.*

Check your grammar

Look at the pictures make sentences with *going to*.

1 She's going to throw the ball.

1 throw the ball   **3** kick a ball

2 sit down   **4** play tennis

104

⑯ Determiners

We use *too many* before countable nouns and *too much* before uncountable nouns.

*I have **too many** books.*

*There's **too much** traffic in my town.*

We use *enough* before nouns but after adjectives.

*My sister doesn't eat **enough** fruit.*

*Our garden is big **enough**.*

Check your grammar

Make sentences with *too many*/*too much* or *enough* and the word in brackets.

1 Please be quiet. You are making too much noise.

1 Please be quiet. You are making … (noise)
2 My sister doesn't go to school. She's not … (old)
4 I'm hungry. I didn't eat … (breakfast)
5 My bag is heavy. There are … in it. (books)
6 I'm not going swimming. It's not … (warm)

⑰ Present passive

We use the passive when we do not know or it is not important who or what does something.

*This bottle **is made** from plastic.*

*Where **are** these vegetables **grown**?*

*This door **is locked** at night.*

Compare the active and passive form:

Active	Passive
*I **lock** this door at night.*	*This door **is locked** at night.*

Notice the form of the present passive:

is/are + past participle

This bottle **is made** from plastic.

Check your grammar

Make sentences with the present passive and these words.

1 Football is played all around the world.

1 football/play/all around the world
2 cheese/make/from milk
3 grapes/grow/in Spain and Italy
4 bridges/build/from steel
5 this key/use/a lot

⑱ *must, mustn't* (obligation)

We use *must* when there is an obligation to do something and *mustn't* when there is an obligation to not do something.

*You **must wear** a crash helmet when you ride a motorcycle.*

*We **mustn't eat** or **drink** in the classroom.*

Affirmative sentences:

I **must work**.
You **must work**.
He **must work**.
She **must work**.
It **must work**.
We **must work**.
You **must work**.
They **must work**.

Negative sentences:

Full form	Short form
I **must not work**.	I **mustn't work**.
You **must not work**.	You **mustn't work**.
He **must not work**.	He **mustn't work**.
She **must not work**.	She **mustn't work**.
It **must not work**.	It **mustn't work**.
We **must not work**.	We **mustn't work**.
You **must not work**.	You **mustn't work**.
They **must not work**.	You **mustn't work**.

Check your grammar

Match the sentences in A with the words in B. Use *must* to make sentences from the words.

1 You're very ill. You must see a doctor.

	A		B
1	You're very ill.	a	You/come/to it
2	I'm tired.	b	You/tidy/it
3	We are bored.	c	You/see/a doctor
4	Your room is untidy.	d	I/go/to bed
5	I'm having a party.	e	We/run
6	We're late for school.	f	We/do/something exciting

Irregular verbs

Present simple	Past simple	Past Participle	Present simple	Past simple	Past Participle
be	was/were	been	leave	left	left
become	became	become	make	made	made
begin	began	begun	meet	met	met
break	broke	broken	put on	put on	put on
bring	brought	brought	read	read	read
build	built	built	ride	rode	ridden
buy	bought	bought	run	ran	run
choose	chose	chosen	say	said	said
do	did	done	see	saw	seen
drink	drank	drunk	send	sent	sent
drive	drove	driven	shoot	shot	shot
eat	ate	eaten	sit	sat	sat
feed	fed	fed	sleep	slept	slept
find	found	found	speak	spoke	spoken
fly	flew	flown	spend	spent	spent
forget	forgot	forgotten	swim	swam	swum
get	got	got	take	took	taken
go	went	gone	throw	threw	thrown
hang out	hung out	hung out	understand	understood	understood
have	had	had	wake up	woke up	woken up
hit	hit	hit	wear	wore	worn
hurt	hurt	hurt	win	won	won
learn	learnt	learnt	write	wrote	written

Word lists

Module 1

Lesson 1

Amish ('ɑmɪʃ)
back in time (bæk ɪn taɪm)
bear (animal) (beə)
bridge (brɪdʒ)
buggy ('bʌgi)
clap (klæp)
creek (kriːk)
diver ('daɪvə)
farmer ('fɑːmə)
field (fiːld)
garden ('gɑːdn)
hedgehog ('hedʒ,hɒg)
hibernate ('haɪbə,neɪt)
horse-drawn ('hɔːs,drɔːn)
human ('hjuːmən)
modern ('mɒdə(r)n)
neighbour ('neɪbə)
river ('rɪvə)
swimmer ('swɪmə)
traditional (trə'dɪʃ(ə)nəl)
walk away (,wɔːk ə'weɪ)
worry ('wʌri)

Lesson 2

cinema ('sɪnəmə)
come back (,kʌm 'bæk)
dentist ('dentɪst)
diary ('daɪəri)
go away (,gəʊ ə'weɪ)
hers (hɜːz)
his (hɪz)
match (mætʃ)
mine (maɪn)
mobile (phone) ('məʊ,baɪl (fəʊn))
netball ('net,bɔːl)
ours (aʊəz)
practise ('præktɪs)
right now ('raɪt ,naʊ)
sketch (sketʃ)
theirs (ðeəz)
watch (wɒtʃ)
yours (jɔːz)

Lesson 3

beautiful ('bjuːtəfl)
big (bɪg)
cheap (tʃiːp)
comfortable ('kʌmftəbl)
expensive (ɪk'spensɪv)

horrible ('hɒrəbl)
interesting ('ɪntrəstɪŋ)
large (lɑːdʒ)
messy ('mesi)
new (njuː)
nice (naɪs)
old (əʊld)
pattern ('pætə(r)n)
price (praɪs)
right (raɪt)
shirt (ʃɜːt)
size (saɪz)
small (smɔːl)
tidy ('taɪdi)
vase (vɑːs)

Lesson 4

angry ('æŋri)
aquarium (ə'kweəriəm)
back and forth ('bæk ənd ,fɔːθ)
cage (keɪdʒ)
cardboard ('kɑːd,bɔːd)
chicken bone ('tʃɪkɪn ,bəʊn)
dog biscuit ('dɒg ,bɪskɪt)
feed (fiːd)
fly (flaɪ)
gerbil ('dʒɜːbl)
mice (maɪs)
parrot ('pærət)
sawdust ('sɔː,dʌst)
seed (siːd)
snake (sneɪk)
stroke (strəʊk)
swish (swɪʃ)
tail (teɪl)
treat (triːt)
upset ('ʌpset)

Module 1 Extra Special

coach (kəʊtʃ)
ferry ('feri)
finally ('faɪn(ə)li)
first (fɜːst)
next (nekst)
ticket ('tɪkɪt)

Module 2

Lesson 5

break (breɪk)
cheer (tʃɪə)
cycling ('saɪklɪŋ)

disaster (dɪˈzɑːstə)
exhibition (ˌeksɪˈbɪʃn)
fall over (ˌfɔːl ˈəʊvə)
javelin (ˈdʒævəlɪn)
jump (dʒʌmp)
long jump (ˈlɒŋ ˌdʒʌmp)
medal (ˈmedl)
obstacle course (ˈɒbstəkl ˌkɔːs)
race (reɪs)
rope (rəʊp)
run (rʌn)
swim (swɪm)
tennis racket (ˈtenɪs ˌrækɪt)
throw (θrəʊ)
twist (twɪst)

Lesson 6
bone (bəʊn)
bury (ˈberi)
clothes line (ˈkləʊðz ˌlaɪn)
flower (ˈflaʊə)
flowerbed (ˈflaʊəˌbed)
flowerpot (ˈflaʊəˌpɒt)
hammock (ˈhæmək)
hang up (ˌhæŋ ˈʌp)
hole (həʊl)
lawn (lɔːn)
mow (məʊ)
plant (plɑːnt)
play with (ˈpleɪ ˌwɪð)
skip (skɪp)
toy (tɔɪ)
tree (triː)
washing (ˈwɒʃɪŋ)
water (ˈwɔːtə)

Lesson 7
alarm (əˈlɑːm)
amazing (əˈmeɪzɪŋ)
bark (ˈbɑːk)
come off (ˌkʌm ˈɒf)
embarrassing (ɪmˈbærəsɪŋ)
fall off (ˌfɔːl ˈɒf)
football boot (ˈfʊtbɔːl ˌbuːt)
goal (gəʊl)
hero (ˈhɪərəʊ)
important (ɪmˈpɔːtnt)
loudly (ˈlaʊdli)
noise (nɔɪz)
on fire (ˌɒn ˈfaɪə)
put out (ˌpʊt ˈaʊt)
referee (ˌrefəˈriː)
saucepan (ˈsɔːspən)
save a life (ˈseɪv ə ˌlaɪf)
slippers (ˈslɪpəs)
smoke (sməʊk)
story (ˈstɔːri)
the score (ˌðə ˈskɔː)
whistle (ˈwɪsl)

Lesson 8
able-bodied (ˌeɪbl ˈbɒdid)
actress (ˈæktrəs)
amputation (ˌæmpjʊˈteɪʃn)
artificial leg (ˌɑːtɪˈfɪʃl ˌleg)
athlete (ˈæθliːt)
attack (əˈtæk)
bite off (ˈbaɪt ˌɒf)
championship (ˈtʃæmpiənʃɪp)
double (ˈdʌbl)
drama (ˈdrɑːmə)
dyslexic (dɪsˈleksɪk)
inspiration (ˌɪnspəˈreɪʃn)
knees (niːs)
model (ˈmɒdl)
shark (ʃɑːk)
softball (ˈsɒftˌbɔːl)
sports foundation (ˈspɔːts faʊnˌdeɪʃn)
surfing (ˈsɜːfɪŋ)
trilogy (ˈtrɪlədʒi)
university (ˌjuːnɪˈvɜːsəti)

Module 2 Extra Special
beans (biːnz)
blanket (ˈblæŋkɪt)
camping (ˈkæmpɪŋ)
cricket (ˈkrɪkɪt)
definitely (ˈdef(ə)nətli)
electric (ɪˈlektrɪk)
fox (fɒks)
gymnastics (dʒɪmˈnæstɪks)
natural (ˈnætʃ(ə)rəl)
rounders (ˈraʊndəz)
rugby (ˈrʌgbi)
sausage (ˈsɒsɪdʒ)
stars (stɑːs)
tent (tent)
torch (tɔːtʃ)

Module 3

Lesson 9
aeroplane (ˈeərəˌpleɪn)
bus (bʌs)
castle (ˈkɑːsl)
cheese (tʃiːz)
Chinese (ˌtʃaɪˈniːz)
ever (evə)
frog (frɒg)
hip hop (ˈhɪp ˌhɒp)
igloo (ˈɪgluː)
leaf (leaves) (liːf (liːvz))
Mexican (ˈmeksɪkən)
never (ˈnevə)
play tennis (ˈpleɪ ˌtenɪs)
pop (pɒp)
rainbow (ˈreɪnˌbəʊ)
rock (rɒk)

smelly ('smeli)
Spanish ('spænɪʃ)
spinach ('spɪnɪdʒ)
(take) exam ((teɪk) ɪg'zæm)
(take) test ((teɪk) test)
train (treɪn)
zoo (zuː)

Lesson 10

brave (breɪv)
desert ('dezət)
elephant ('elɪfənt)
horse (hɔːs)
king (kɪŋ)
make (a film) (meɪk (ə fɪlm))
moon (muːn)
mountain ('maʊntɪn)
queen (kwiːn)
ride (raɪd)
sail (seɪl)
ski (skiː)
world record (ˌwɜːld 'rekɔːd)

Lesson 11

annoying (ə'nɔɪɪŋ)
back (bæk)
best pal (ˌbest 'pæl)
busy ('bɪzi)
change (tʃeɪndʒ)
DIY (ˌdiː aɪ 'waɪ)
gorgeous ('gɔːdʒəs)
hairstyle ('heəˌstaɪl)
hurt (hɜːt)
kitten ('kɪtn)
purple ('pɜːpl)
sleepover ('sliːpˌəʊvə)
uniform ('juːnɪˌfɔːm)
vet (vet)

Lesson 12

celebration (ˌselə'breɪʃn)
dance (dɑːns)
fisherman ('fɪʃəmən)
flood (flʌd)
future ('fjuːtʃə)
happy ('hæpi)
independence (ˌɪndɪ'pendəns)
island ('aɪlənd)
land (lænd)
language ('læŋgwɪdʒ)
low (ləʊ)
net (net)
pork (pɔːk)
sad (sæd)
sea (siː)
share (ʃeə)
song (sɒŋ)
stilts (stɪlts)

tiny ('taɪni)

Module 4

Lesson 13

audience ('ɔːdiəns)
bronze (brɒnz)
costume ('kɒstjuːm)
dread (dred)
entertain (ˌentə'teɪn)
gold (gəʊld)
guitar (gɪ'tɑː)
judge (dʒʌdʒ)
microphone ('maɪkrəˌfəʊn)
pilot ('paɪlət)
prediction (prɪ'dɪkʃn)
silver ('sɪlvə)
stage (steɪdʒ)
stranger ('streɪndʒə)
talent show ('tælənt ʃəʊ)

Lesson 14

accordion (ə'kɔːdiən)
amp (æmp)
aspirin ('æsprɪn)
borrow ('bɒrəʊ)
calculator ('kælkjʊˌleɪtə)
could (kʊd)
double bass (ˌdʌbl 'beɪs)
flute (fluːt)
keyboards ('kiːˌbɔːds)
map (mæp)
offer ('ɒfə)
recorder (rɪ'kɔːdə)
request (rɪ'kwest)
turn up (ˌtɜːn 'ʌp)
violin (ˌvaɪə'lɪn)

Lesson 15

circus ('sɜːkəs)
classic ('klæsɪk)
comedy ('kɒmədi)
entertainer (ˌentə'teɪnə)
festival ('festɪvl)
fireworks ('faɪəwɜːks)
folk music ('fəʊk ˌmjuːzɪk)
jazz (dʒæz)
mime (maɪm)
opera ('ɒp(ə)rə)
puppet ('pʌpɪt)
spectacular (spek'tækjʊlə)
suggestion (sə'dʒestʃ(ə)n)

Lesson 16

corridor ('kɒrɪˌdɔː)
drums (drʌms)
exhausted (ɪg'zɔːstɪd)

library ('laɪbrəri)
musical ('mjuːzɪkl)
performing arts (pərˌfɔːmɪŋ 'ɑːts)
state-funded (ˌsteɪt'fʌndɪd)
stretch (stretʃ)
successful (sək'sesfl)

Module 4 Extra Special
aquarium (ə'kweəriəm)
chess (tʃes)
chimpanzee (ˌtʃɪmpæn'ziː)
expert ('ekspɜːt)
gadget ('gædʒɪt)
jet (dʒet)
open-air (ˌəʊpən 'eə)
submarine ('sʌbməriːn)
swimming costume ('swɪmɪŋ ˌkɒstjuːm)
zookeeper ('zuːˌkiːpə)

Module 5

Lesson 17
a cold (ə 'kəʊld)
a cough (ə 'kɒf)
a headache (ə 'hedeɪk)
a sore throat (ə 'sɔː ˌθrəʊt)
a stomach ache (ə 'stʌmək ˌeɪk)
a temperature (ə 'temprɪˌtʃə)
apple ('æpl)
flu (fluː)
ill (ɪl)
medicine ('medsn)
remote (rɪ'məʊt)
water (wɔːtə)

Lesson 18
bull (bʊl)
countryside ('kʌntriˌsaɪd)
dark (dɑːk)
games (geɪms)
hungry ('hʌŋgri)
insect spray ('ɪnsekt ˌspreɪ)
lost (lɒst)

Lesson 19
advice (əd'vaɪs)
birthday ('bɜːθdeɪ)
church (tʃɜːtʃ)
coffee ('kɒfi)
custom ('kʌstəm)
dirty ('dɜːti)
dream (driːm)
hiccup ('hɪkʌp)
immediately (ɪ'miːdiətli)
meal (miːl)
pat (pæt)
plate (pleɪt)

present ('preznt)
rude (ruːd)
school (skuːl)
sheep (ʃiːp)
sneeze (sniːz)
snore (snɔː)
stare (steə)
visitor ('vɪzɪtə)
wedding ('wedɪŋ)
wet (wet)

Lesson 20
climb (klaɪm)
crawl (krɔːl)
dangerous ('deɪndʒərəs)
downstream ('daʊnˌstriːm)
flames (fleɪmz)
forest ('fɒrɪst)
jungle ('dʒʌŋgl)
lightning ('laɪtnɪŋ)
path ('pɑːθ)
puncture ('pʌŋktʃə)
safe (seɪf)
shout (ʃɔːt)
stand (stænd)
storm (stɔːm)
strike (straɪk)
survival (sə'vaɪvl)
upstream (ʌp'striːm)
voice (vɔɪs)

Module 5 Extra Special
camel ('kæml)
canyon ('kænjən)
gondola ('gɒndələ)
kangaroo (ˌkæŋgə'ruː)
kilt (kɪlt)
Portuguese (ˌpɔːtʃʊ'giːz)
tower ('taʊə)
tulip ('tjuːlɪp)
volcano (vɒl'keɪnəʊ)

Module 6

Lesson 21
broom (bruːm)
drill (drɪl)
hammer ('hæmə)
ladder ('lædə)
paint (peɪnt)
soup (suːp)
spill (spɪl)
toolbox ('tuːl ˌbɒks)
trip over (ˌtrɪp 'əʊvə)
wallpaper ('wɔːlˌpeɪpə)
watch out (ˌwɒtʃ 'aʊt)
window ('wɪndəʊ)

Lesson 22

caravan ('kærə,væn)
cottage ('kɒtɪdʒ)
cupboard ('kʌbəd)
exciting (ɪk'saɪtɪŋ)
farm (fɑːm)
furniture ('fɜːnɪtʃə)
lighthouse ('laɪt,haʊs)
Outback [of Australia] ('aʊt,bæk (ɒf ɒ'streɪliə))
peaceful ('piːsfl)
radio ('reɪdiəʊ)
ranch (rɑːntʃ)
sofa ('səʊfə)
stairs (steəs)
tourist ('tʊərɪst)
traffic ('træfɪk)
vehicle ('viːɪkl)
view (vjuː)

Lesson 23

billion ('bɪljən)
build (bɪld)
eco-village ('iːləʊ,vɪlɪdʒ)
electricity (ɪ,lek'trɪsəti)
energy ('enədʒi)
fleece (fliːs)
laundry ('lɔːndri)
melt (melt)
million ('mɪljən)
per cent (pə'sent)
power ('paʊə)
produce (prə'djuːs)
recycle (riː'saɪkl)
reuse (riː'juːz)
share (ʃeə)
string (strɪŋ)
tonne (tʌn)
top (tɒp)
wind turbine ('wɪnd ,tɜːbaɪn)

Lesson 24

alien ('eɪliən)
chicken ('tʃɪkɪn)
explorer (ɪk'splɔːrə)
goat (gəʊt)
researcher (rɪ'sɜːtʃə)
rocket ('rɒkɪt)
valley ('væli)

Module 6 – Extra Special

accident ('æksɪd(ə)nt)
cocoa bean ('kəʊkəʊ ,biːn)
omelette ('ɒmlət)
paint pot ('peɪnt ,pɒt)
paintbrush ('peɪnt,brʌʃ)
sand (sænd)

Module 7

Lesson 25

crash helmet ('kræʃ ,helmɪt)
crossroads ('krɒs,rəʊdz)
cycle ('saɪkl)
cycle lane ('saɪkl ,leɪn)
excuse me (ɪk'skjuːz ,miː)
motorbike ('məʊtə,baɪk)
must (mʌst)
park (pɑːk)
parking meter ('pɑːkɪŋ ,miːtə)
pavement ('peɪvmənt)
pedestrian crossing (pə,destriən 'krɒsɪŋ)
straight on (,streɪt 'ɒn)
traffic light ('træfɪk ,laɪt)
traffic sign ('træfɪk ,saɪn)
traffic warden ('træfɪk ,wɔːdn)

Lesson 26

for (fɔː)
full name (,fʊl 'neɪm)
guard (gɑːd)
identity (aɪ'dentɪ,ti)
licence ('laɪsns)
mistake (mɪ'steɪk)
passport ('pɑːspɔːt)
secret agent (,siːkrət 'eɪdʒ(ə)nt)
since (sɪns)
world famous (,wɜːld 'feɪməs)

Lesson 27

balcony ('bælkəni)
belt (belt)
chords (kɔːdz)
grape (greɪp)
Highlands ('haɪləndz)
karate (kə'rɑːti)
Malaysian (mə'leɪsiə)
peanut ('piːnʌt)
pot (pɒt)
tomato (tə'mɑːtəʊ)
typical ('tɪpɪkl)

Lesson 28

cave (keɪv)
cowboy ('kaʊ,bɔɪ)
delicious (dɪ'lɪʃəs)
lake (leɪk)
native ('neɪtɪv)
pineapple ('paɪn,æpl)
rent (rent)
roof (ruːf)
teepee ('tiːpiː)

Module 7 – Extra Special

concert ('kɒnsət)
poetry ('pəʊɪtri)

Macmillan Education
Between Towns Road, Oxford OX4 3PP
A division of Macmillan Publishers Limited
Companies and representatives throughout the world

ISBN 978-0-230-53378-3

Text © Colin Granger and Katharine Stannett 2010
Design and illustration © Macmillan Publishers Limited 2010

Original design by Wild Apple Design
Page make-up by Giles Davies
Illustrated by Adrian Barclay, Russ Daff, Wes Lowe, Chris Pavely,
Baz Rowell, Mark Ruffle, Simon Rumble, Martin Sanders, Jorge
Santillon, Lisa Smith, Simon Smith, Mark Turner and Gary Wing
Cover design by Designers Collective; background image by iStock

Authors' acknowledgements
The authors would like to thank the editorial team at Macmillan,
especially Dulcie Fry, Madeleine Williamson and Mireille Yanow,
for their hard work, good humour and professionalism. Katherine
Stannett would also like to give special thanks to her inspirational
co-author, Colin, for his constant encouragement. Finally, she
would also like to express love and thanks to her husband, Jim, and
her daughters, Martha and Jess, for their patience and support.

The publishers would like to thank Magdalena Kondro, Xanthe Sturt
Taylor, Aniela Baranowska, Lidia Domańska, Jarmila Fictumova,
Maria Goretaya, Paulina Grabowska, Aileen Graham, Gréta
Korpádiová, Katarzyna Oberda, Anna Petrenkova, Karolina Siupa,
Katie Stephens, Marta Studniarek, Renata Szwaj, Miriam Vaswani
and Ewa Wódkowska.

The authors and publishers would like to thank the following for
permission to reproduce their photographic materials:
Alamy/ blinkwinkel p70(c), Alamy/ Rob Cousins p72(br),
Alamy/ Shaun Cunningham pp6(br), 89(11), Alamy/ Gist Images
pp84(tr), 89(15), Alamy/ Jeff Greenberg pp7(tr), 14(b), 58(tr),
88(2), Alamy/ Iconotec p77(cocoa), Alamy/ Janine Wiedel
Photolibrary p41(t), Alamy/ David Kadlubowski p64(j), Alamy/ Jim
Lane p22(c), Alamy/ Lenscap p45(tr), Alamy/ Mediablitzimages
UK Ltd p41(b), Alamy/ Motoring Picture Library p77(car),
Alamy/ Nordic Photos p64(c), Alamy/ Owaki/Kulla pp68(tl),
88(12a), Alamy/ PCL p47, Alamy/ Photodisc p87(c), Alamy/ Emil
Pozar p77(hair), Alamy/ Simon Reddy p82(cl), Alamy/ Doug
Steley p68(b), 89(12d), Alamy/ Steppenwolf pp68(c), 89(12b),
Alamy/ Travelshots.com p64(f), Alamy/ Rob Walls p23(b),
Alamy/ Doug Wilson p64(e);
Brand X/ pp64(i), 68(tl insert), 70(br), 87(tl);
Corbis/ pp17, 64(a), 77(grass), Corbis/ Atlantide Phototravel
p84(br), Corbis/ Neville Elder p72(bl), Corbis/ Brooke Fasani
p48(bc), Corbis/ Image Source p87(bl), Corbis/ Rob Lewine pp72(l),
89(13), Corbis/ Lawrence Manning p45(tl), Corbis/ Gideon Mendel
pp70(bl), 75, Corbis/ Robert Michael p29(t), Corbis/ Michael Prince
pp6(tr), 14(c), 58(b), 88(1);
Digital Stock/ p64(b), Digital Stock/ Corbis p64(h);
Fotolibra/ Mark Fearon pp68(t), 89(12c), Fotolibra/ Robert Ho
p82(br), Fotolibra/ Avi Kallan p77(wood);
Getty Images/ pp 24(l), 24(r), 88(4), Getty Images/ Blasius
Erlinger p22(t), Getty Images/ Sylvain Grandadam p7(br), Getty
Images/ VEER Third Eye Images p58(3);
Image Source/ pp23(cl), 64(d), 64(g), 68(b insert), 68(c insert);
Lodgepole Gallery and Tipi Village, USA p85;
Lonely Planet/ David Creedy p6(bl);
Macmillan Publishers Ltd/ David Tolley p45(bl);
Macmillan Readers cover/ *Nelson Mandela* Getty/Tom Stoddart p87
NationalGeographicStock.com/ Dean Conger/photo illustration by
Macmillan Publishers Ltd p84(c);
NPL/ Jane Burton p22(b);
PA Photos/ p25(b);
Photodisc pp13, 23(tl), 58(2), 68(t insert), 72(tr), 77(sand);
Photolibrary/ age fotostock p82(tl), Photolibrary/ Liane Cary
p29(c), Photolibrary/ Fresh Food Images pp38, 77(omelette),
Photolibrary/ Garden Picture Library p82(tr), Photolibrary/ Dennis
Macdonald p58(1), Photolibrary/ Mauritius p77(water),
Photolibrary/ Red Chopsticks pp6(tl), 14(t), 58(tl, 88(10),
Photolibrary/ Zen Shui p45(br), 69, Photolibrary/ Stockbyte p73,
Photolibrary/ Wave Royalty Free p70(t);
Punchstock/ Digital Vision p23(cr), Punchstock/ Thinkstock p49;
Rex Features/ Alix/Phanie p77(plastic), Rex Features/ Nick Cunard
pp48(c), 48(bl), Rex Features/ IBL p88(9), Rex Features/ Image
Source p23(tr), Rex Features/ Elinor Jones p53, Rex Features/ Ken
McKay p25(t), Rex Features/ Richard Young p91;
Stockbyte/ pp29(b), 82(bl), 87(r).

Commissioned photography by:
Paul Bricknell pp8, 18, 26, 46, 56, 57, 62, 82 (portrait), 83, 88(8).

The author and publishers are grateful for permission to reprint the
following copyright material:
We Are The Champions – Words and Music by Freddie Mercury,
© 1977, reproduced by permission of Queen Music Limited, London
W8 5SW;
Have You Ever Seen The Rain – Words and Music by John C Fogerty,
© 1970, reproduced by kind permission of Prestige Music Limited;
I Have A Dream – Words and Music by Benny Andersson and Björn
Ulvaeus, © 1979, reproduced by kind permission of Bocu Music
Limited.

Printed and bound in Thailand

2015 2014 2013 2012 2011
10 9 8 7 6 5 4 3 2